# PRAYER MADE SIMPLE

God moved my mountain!
He can move yours too!

Terry Manley

WESTBOW·
PRESS
A DIVISION OF THOMAS NELSON
& ZONDERVAN

WestBow Press books may be ordered through booksellers or by contacting:

WestBow Press
A Division of Thomas Nelson & Zondervan
1663 Liberty Drive
Bloomington, IN 47403
www.westbowpress.com
1 (866) 928-1240

ISBN: 978-1-4908-6046-6 (sc)

Library of Congress Control Number: 2014920493

Print information available on the last page.

WestBow Press rev. date: 03/06/2015

# DEDICATION

This book is dedicated to all generations of family who preceded me, who lovingly sowed countless seeds of faith, honoring our Almighty Father in heaven. They opened their hearts to receive the Word of God, humbly demonstrating their faith through prayers, actions and words that glorified Him. Because of their great faith and devotion to God, my loved ones and I are the recipients of His divine blessings.

May we all plant seeds of faith for *all* our future generations, faithfully "praying forward" beautiful family blessings through hope and conversations with Almighty God.

# ACKNOWLEDGMENTS

I humbly and prayerfully acknowledge God our Father in heaven, who gives us many gifts: His unconditional love, mercy, forgiveness, and divine grace, just to name a few. I thank the Almighty Father for blessing me with this beautiful life, this brief moment in time, where each day I can demonstrate my faith and love in Him through His beloved Son, Jesus Christ, and by the power of the Holy Spirit that lives within me. I know the Almighty Father has a purpose for my life. I focus my eyes of faith on fulfilling that purpose so that I may share eternity with Him and with those whom I care deeply about, all for the glory and honor of our Lord, Jesus Christ.

God places people in your path for a specific purpose; it's all part of His great plan. Sometimes it is to make a difference in their life and sometimes it is so they can make a difference in yours. God has placed two extraordinary people in my path who helped to change the course of my life: my loving husband Steve, and my dear friend Pam Watson. I am eternally grateful to God for choosing these two special people to grace my life.

# CONTENTS

# CONTENTS

# INTRODUCTION

I quickly became good friends with Pam Watson through our love for horses. During our peaceful trail rides, Pam would share inspiring stories about her faith and about how prayer makes her life more enriched, more powerful. She would share her conversations with God. I found myself amazed as she told me how those conversations brought about beautiful answers to her prayers. It turned out we shared two interests: our love for horses, and more importantly, our love for God. Pam's friendship reignited a passion inside of me: my *relationship* with God. That spark was the beginning of this extraordinary journey, bringing my family and me closer to our Heavenly Father, His Son, Jesus Christ, and the Holy Spirit in a powerful way.

Pam kept telling me to write my prayers down. She would beautifully describe how to "wrap" my prayer around God's Word by including with my prayer an inspiring Scripture from the Bible. I loved the sound of it![1]

I found my old journal, which I hadn't picked up in many years. I dusted it off and opened it. The last entry was dated January, 2001, twelve years earlier. At the time, I was on a mission to manifest the "ideal man" for myself. My heart yearned to meet the *right* man. I filled almost two pages with *very specific* qualities he would need to possess. There was no room for speculation. I remember sitting with my journal almost every morning, reading these two pages and praying that someday this man would appear before me. God heard my heart, my simple prayers, and four short months later Steve, my husband, entered my life.

When I looked back and read my outline, my little prayer, I realized that Steve possessed every single quality. *Every one.* Amazing! I honestly believe God heard me. God's divine intervention brought us together. Steve's actions, words and love have taught me many things: among them compassion, sincerity, humility, honesty, and generosity. In admiration, I watch his selfless actions daily. I am blessed to have him in my life; he is my best friend.

Writing prayers down works; I experienced it firsthand! I made a commitment to pick up where I had left off, this time including God's Word with my prayers.

My family was in the midst of a very difficult period when I decided to start writing down my prayers. We were faced with an assortment of hardships: health, business, family. God's timing was perfect!

Prayers were written; I spent quiet time with God's Word. Amazing conversations opened up between God and me. As I poured my heart out to Him, He heard my prayers! I began to check them off one by one as He answered them. God is so faithful.

God's love for me and His willingness to help me became so apparent. I reached out to all my loved ones who were facing their own set of challenges and sent them their very own journals. Conversations with God are so exciting; I wanted them all to experience their own personal, profound and powerful relationship with Him. To help them get started, I included in their journal one or two Scriptures from the Bible and a prayer I had written specifically for their circumstances. I attempted to give them a few examples, hoping this would become their "prayer book." Surprisingly, most of them could not get started. They never wrote in their books. They didn't know where or how to begin; they were stuck. I have to admit I was a little disappointed.

Then my mom expressed an interest in having a prayer book. Her prayer book would be different - *simple*. She wanted more examples of prayers with an assortment of Scriptures. I wrote the prayers for her so she would only have to insert names or specific details, making the prayers personal for her. As she prayed for different loved ones or different situations, she would simply change the name or circumstances. The chapters just started growing and growing. The Holy Spirit had so much to say and used my pen and my availability to "pour out." I was astounded. Once it was complete, I gave my hand written book to my mom in hopes of encouraging her to open a dialogue between her and God.

One day, my mom opened up her prayer book to the chapter on "Patience and Perseverance" and prayed. She called me with a praise report. She felt her prayer was answered. Halleluiah! She was not only using the book; she was hearing from God! My mom loves her prayer book and keeps it beside her Bible. It provides another avenue to approach God and worship Him in a deep and powerful way, hearing His voice, His Word, His direction, His truth - *personally*.

May *PRAYER MADE SIMIPLE* encourage and inspire you through His Word, not mine! God is capable of creating great change in your life! Take the first step and open up a dialogue with Him. He is waiting to hear from you. Let's get started!

# PART I - LESSONS OF FAITH FOR YOU!

The chapters in Part I of *PRAYER MADE SIMPLE* are the significant and beautiful lessons of faith I learned from the Holy Spirit throughout my journey, which *greatly* influenced how I pray. I share them with you and hope they strengthen your daily prayer life as well.

During my journey to know God better, I realized I had never taken the time to deliberately, specifically and intentionally invite Jesus into my life. My faith in God just was not enough. Failing to ask Jesus into my life as my personal Lord and Savior meant I was missing out on God's gift of salvation through HIS grace. When I made this commitment, I became a new creation in Christ and part of God's family.

As you continue your faith walk with Christ, *be sure* you've prayed to receive Jesus into your life. If you can't remember ever doing so, please pray right now!

> For God so loved the world that he gave his one and only son, that whoever believes in him shall not perish but have eternal life.
> **John 3:16**

### "Salvation" Prayer

*Thank You Father for giving me Jesus, Your Beloved Son, my Lord and Savior. I confess I am a sinner Father, and I am sorry. As I turn away from my sins, I ask for Your Divine mercy and forgiveness.*

*I profess my faith in Jesus, Who died for my sins and was raised on the third day. I give my heart over to Jesus, to take control and be the Lord of my life. Thank You Jesus for Your love and sacrifice.*

*Almighty God, I thank You for Your gift of salvation, that through my faith and trust in Your Son, Jesus Christ, You forgive me, and accept me into Your kingdom of life. In Jesus' name I pray.*

*Amen*

# 1 - START A CONVERSATION

The Bible is full of Scriptures with messages, lessons, wisdom, knowledge and understanding. Every answer you could ever need is in the Bible. There are so many pearls of wisdom just waiting for you. It is like your own personal "How-To Manual." The Bible teaches you how to love and honor God, how to receive salvation, how to live a joyful life, how to love yourself, how to love others, how to be generous, how to pray, how to give thanks in all circumstances. You name it, the Bible has it! Show God how much you love Him: read His Word; live His Word.

The Lord replied: "Write down the revelation and make it plain on tablets so that a herald may run with it."

**Habakkuk 2:2**

This was one of the first Scriptures my dear friend Pam shared with me. It doesn't get much clearer than this when God himself instructs us to write down our prayers. How powerful! God grants us the opportunity to ask specifically for what we desire.

May he give you the desire of your heart and make all your plans succeed.

**Psalm 20:4**

Talking with God through prayer is vital to having a strong and intimate relationship with Him. When you include Scripture, God's Word, with your prayers, you are totally engaged in a two-way conversation, and it is beautiful. You draw spiritual strength from God while revealing to Him the attitude of your heart – just one way to worship Him.

3

First you look for a Scripture in the Bible that speaks to your heart based on the intent of your prayer; this is *God speaking to you.* Then you compose your prayer in great detail, being very specific; this is *you speaking to God.* You reflect on both your prayer and the hope and truth you find in the Scripture, "wrapping" your prayer around God's Word.

If you aren't sure where to begin, *PRAYER MADE SIMPLE* has done all of this for you! In Part II of this book, the Scriptures and prayers are waiting for you. All you have to do is insert specific names and circumstances into the prayers to make them your own. Choose a Scripture that speaks to your heart and your situation, and meditate on God's Word and your prayer together. It doesn't get any easier than this!

Rejoice always, pray continually, give
thanks in all circumstances; for this is
God's will for you in Christ Jesus.

**1 Thessalonians 5:16–18**

If you already have a daily prayer practice in place, consider making God's Word part of it. Be thankful and praise God for His love and grace. Let Him know how important He is to you. Pray with all your heart and don't just ask God for help; *pray specifically.* Whether it be for a particular job, health, forgiveness, or to give thanks, just praise Him for who He is. Be specific in what you are praying for and <u>write</u> <u>it</u> <u>down!</u>

If you don't have a daily prayer practice, I hope this book will encourage you to begin one today. Believe; have faith and trust in God. As your relationship with God strengthens; He will help you transform your ordinary into *extraordinary!*

# 2 - PRAISE AND WORSHIP

God loves you in a mighty way. He is the Giver of *all* gifts and throughout the Bible you are instructed to worship and praise Him for all the many gifts He has given you. He gave you His Son, Jesus Christ; there is no greater gift! He gave you The Holy Spirit. He gave you life.

Rick Warren, Author of *The Purpose Driven Life*, says "Worship is your spirit responding to God's Spirit." God wants your spirit to communicate with Him, and He wants you to be honest and sincere. If you have questions, God wants to hear them; if you have doubts, God wants to know them; He doesn't want you to say what *you think He wants to hear*. God wants your honesty. God is reading your heart so you should worship Him in truth.[2]

Jesus said:

> "God is Spirit, so those who worship him
> must worship in spirit and in truth."
>
> **John 4:24 NLT**

When you worship God, you must be willing to surrender fully to the Holy Spirit, to entrust your life to God. We'll talk more in detail about surrendering in Chapter 4. Just know, when you give yourself entirely to Him and don't hold back, you worship Him in the deepest, most profound way.

God wants you to obey His commandments and carry out His Will through His plan for you. He wants you to trust Him, pray to Him, talk to Him, read the Bible, feel His Word. Through all this you show God how much you really love Him.

Come, let us bow down in worship, let us kneel before
the Lord our Maker; for he is our God and we are the
people of his pasture, the flock under his care.

**Psalm 95:6-7**

## "Worship and Glorify" Prayer

*Almighty God,*

*With all my heart, I worship and glorify You. Each day, as I
strive to do Your Will, Father, I ask the Holy Spirit to guide me
and fill me with grace, wisdom, and understanding. My heart
is focused on modeling my life in the image of Your Blessed
Son, Jesus Christ. I pray for continued courage and strength
so I may show You daily, through my words, thoughts, and
actions, how much I adore and honor You.*

*Amen*

Through your prayers, your conversations with God, you praise,
worship, and honor Him. Let God know in your quiet time how
deeply He touches your heart. Let God know throughout your busy
day how deeply He touches your heart. Praise Him when you open
your eyes in the morning and before you close them at night.

From the rising of the sun to the place where it
sets, the name of the Lord is to be praised.

**Psalm 113:3**

Tell God how grateful you are for His unconditional love and for
every day you are given to demonstrate your love and devotion for
Him, through your faith in His Son, Jesus Christ.

I will praise you as long as I live, and in
your name I will lift up my hands.

**Psalm 63:4**

### "Praise God!" Prayer

*Praise God, for You are the mighty One who shows me love in a glorious way! I honor You, Father God; giver of all gifts. I rejoice in Your name. You have blessed me with life, and I am so grateful. I offer up this day to You, Father. May all I do and say magnify the love in my heart for You.*

# 3 - MEET THE HOLY SPIRIT

God, our Father, created the universe. He created me; He created you. The Father wants us to follow Him in all we do; He has a great plan for us. He wants us to obey His Ten Commandments. He is forgiving. We pray to Him. We praise and glorify Him. He sent us His beloved Son, Jesus Christ to save us. We want to spend eternity with Him.

Jesus Christ is the Son of God, our Lord and Savior. Jesus teaches us God's Word. He prayed to God. He served those on earth; He served His Father. He ministered; He empowered. He was humble; He forgave. He died for us and for our sins. He rose from the dead, and He sits at the right hand of the Father. We are made righteous through faith in Him. He holds the key to heaven. He pours out the gift of the Holy Spirit to all believers. He gives us grace; He intercedes for us, hears our prayers and helps us.

I *knew* of the Holy Spirit, but I didn't *know Him*. I read and said His name many times in prayers, and felt Him in me, but I didn't understand exactly what the Holy Spirit's role was. When I took the time to get to know Him, my love for Him deepened in an inexpressible way; my whole world changed.

The Holy Spirit was so significant in helping me to write this book. If you don't know the Holy Spirit personally, I hope by the end of this book you will *want* to know Him. He is waiting patiently to be invited into your heart, into your being. He wants to direct your footsteps, your words…will you let Him?

Who is the Holy Spirit? The Holy Spirit is a divine person. The Holy Spirit is as much God as the Father and the Son. They are all equal: One God revealed in three persons. God is all-powerful; He is everywhere and He is all knowing. It is a hard concept; I guess that's why they call it faith.

We live by faith, not by sight.

**2 Corinthians 5:7**

Benny Hinn, Author of *Good Morning, Holy Spirit,* writes "The Holy Spirit is the Spirit of God the Father and God the Son." The Holy Spirit is the *force*, the *energy*, the *power* behind what the Father commands and what the Son performs. For example, when God directed Jesus to heal someone, Jesus *performed* the healing but the actual healing came by the power of the Holy Spirit. The Holy Spirit *brings to life, brings things into being*; He is the action behind God, who is not able to come to earth.

The Holy Spirit is the voice of God the Father. Hinn adds, "The Holy Spirit is the one who communicates heaven into your heart."

The Bible speaks of so many beautiful, amazing accounts of the power of the Holy Spirit; in fact He "wrote" the Bible. He used men from all walks of life, but every one of them was led by the Holy Spirit.[3]

No prophecy of Scripture came about by the
prophet's own interpretation of things. For
prophecy never had its origin in the human will,
but prophets, though human, spoke from God
as they were carried along by the Holy Spirit.

**2 Peter 1:20-21**

I encourage you to discover more through reading your Bible. You can start anywhere from Genesis to Revelation, and feel just how wonderful and significant the Holy Spirit is.

The Holy Spirit was part of the creation of the Universe.

> The Spirit of God was hovering over the waters. And
> God said, "Let there be light," and there was light.

**Genesis 1:2–3**

Through His power, the Virgin Mary conceived and gave birth to Jesus Christ.

> God sent the angel Gabriel to Nazareth...

> "You will conceive and give birth to a
> son, and you will name him Jesus."

> Mary asked the angel, "But how can
> this happen? I am a virgin."

> The angel replied, "The Holy Spirit will come
> upon you, and the power of the Most High will
> overshadow you. So the baby to be born will be
> holy, and he will be called the Son of God."

**Luke 1:26,31,34–35 NLT**

When Jesus preached, it was *in the power* of the Holy Spirit. When He healed, it was *in the power* of the Holy Spirit. The Holy Spirit filled Him with words and performed the healing. Jesus would not move without the Holy Spirit.

On the night before Jesus died, He promised the apostles that He would send the Holy Spirit from the Father to assist them in spreading the message of God. They would no longer have Jesus to follow but would now turn to the Holy Spirit for guidance, intercession and strength.[4]

We were all given the gift of the Holy Spirit at Pentecost. Since that day, the Holy Spirit represents the Father and the Son, here on earth inside you and me! How wonderful! How glorious! How...God!

Jesus said:

> "I will ask the Father, and he will give you
> another advocate to help you and be with
> you forever – the Spirit of truth."

**John 14:16-17**

What exactly does the Holy Spirit do? The Holy Spirit thinks, feels, communicates and responds. He gives and receives love. His character *is love*. The Holy Spirit can speak to you, and He teaches you how to speak to the Father. He makes decisions, takes sides in disputes, creates, directs, reminds, and hears. He tells you what is yet to come. He is intelligent and good.[5]

> The Holy Spirit produces this kind of fruit in our
> lives: love, joy, peace, patience, kindness, goodness,
> faithfulness, gentleness and self-control.

**Galatians 5:22-23 NLT**

The Holy Spirit is your comforter and counselor. When you accept that your life here on earth is to prepare yourself for eternity, you can better understand why life can be difficult at times. If it weren't, it would be called heaven. When you invite the Holy Spirit into your life, your life has purpose and meaning. Rick Warren says "When life has meaning, you can bear almost anything; without it, nothing is bearable."[6]

> May the God of hope fill you with all joy and peace
> as you trust in him, so that you may overflow
> with hope by the power of the Holy Spirit.

**Romans 15:13**

When you don't know what to pray, the Holy Spirit makes intercession for you. The Holy Spirit will help you put into words your expression of devotion and gratefulness, your requests for help and guidance in all aspects of life for yourself, for those you love, even for complete strangers. The Holy Spirit will also help you to endure while you wait for your prayers to be answered.[7]

> The Holy Spirit helps us in our weakness. For example, we don't know what God wants us to pray for. But the Holy Spirit prays for us with groanings that cannot be expressed in words. And the Father who knows all hearts knows what the Spirit is saying, for the Spirit pleads for us believers in harmony with God's own will.

**Romans 8:26-27 NLT**

I used to think the "little voice" inside me was my intuition. I now believe the Holy Spirit *is* that little voice inside me who speaks to me, guides me, tries to protect me, gives me warnings, and guides me to follow God's path. If you are a believer in Christ, I'm sure your little voice has the same name.

How many times have I said to myself, "I should have followed my intuition, it never steers me wrong." Well, of course, He won't steer me wrong – *it's God speaking!* Can you believe He loves us that much!

The Holy Spirit is so gentle. He never shouts at us, "You dummy, didn't I tell you to do it this way?" He loves us enough to let us learn for ourselves. It is all part of the process of defining our character.

The Holy Spirit wants you to live a life that pleases God. He doesn't want you to think only of yourself and your pleasure; you should ensure that your life is pleasing to God. When you approach life with that goal in mind and accept the help of The Holy Spirit, your life will be transformed.

You are already set up for success, but God has given you the freedom to choose His way or yours; yield to His Spirit, or yield to your flesh.[8]

Although God gives you the freedom of choice, you do not have the freedom from the consequences of your choice.[9] God's plan has you following Him in *all* you do. When you put the emphasis on what pleases God, it helps you in your decision-making process.

> Everything in the world – the lust of the flesh, the lust of the eyes, and the pride of life – comes not from the Father but from the world. The world and its desires pass away, but whoever does the will of God lives forever.

**1 John 2:16-17**

The Holy Spirit is your guarantee of redemption. As you live a spirit-filled life, you begin a transformation, a process that will take your lifetime to complete. What waits for you is an eternity of being in the presence of God, an opportunity to be reunited with loved ones who also received redemption.

> When you believed in Christ, he identified you as his own by giving you the Holy Spirit, whom he promised long ago. The Spirit is God's guarantee that he will give us the inheritance he promised... He did this so we would praise and glorify him.

**Ephesians 1:13-14 NLT**

One of my favorite Scriptures from the Bible is Colossians 1:9-12. It tells us that the Holy Spirit will share with us *everything* we need to know and do in order to fulfill God's Will, God's plan for us. We don't have to guess. We just need to listen and follow. The Holy Spirit blesses us with strength, power, knowledge, endurance, patience and joy, helping us to live a life worthy of the Lord so we may share in His eternal inheritance. What a gift we've all been given. Will you accept the Holy Spirit into your life and follow Him?

We continually ask God to fill you with the knowledge
of his will through all the wisdom and understanding
that the Spirit gives, so that you may live a life worthy
of the Lord and please him in every way: bearing
fruit in every good work, growing in the knowledge
of God, being strengthened with all power, according
to his glorious might so that you may have great
endurance and patience, and giving joyful thanks
to the Father, who has qualified you to share in the
inheritance of his holy people in the kingdom of light.

**Colossians 1:9-12**


As part of your daily prayer practice, take the time to *pause* and ask
God questions; then listen. Hear what *His* plans are for you today.

It is the Lord your God you must follow,
and him you must revere.

**Deuteronomy 13:4**


**"What can I do to serve You?" Prayer**


*Almighty Father,*

*What can I do to serve You today? May the Holy Spirit guide
me today and every day to do Your Will, Heavenly God, shining
His light on my path so I walk confidently in the Spirit. I ask
You to fill me with strength, courage and compassion so that I
may be successful. I ask You this, Father, in Your beloved Son
Jesus Christ's name.*

*Amen*

# 4 - SURRENDER TO THE HOLY SPIRIT

God the Father and God the Son are not here on earth; they are in heaven, but the Holy Spirit is here on this earth *right now!* He is with you *this very moment*, and if you allow Him, He will lead you to salvation. Without the Holy Spirit you'd be left on your own to figure out how to get there. *It just can't happen without Him.*

When the Holy Spirit returns to heaven, He will take with Him those who have been redeemed.[10] Until that day arrives, the Holy Spirit is here to prepare you, but first, you need to take that step of faith and surrender to His Spirit. Surrender your thoughts, words, and desires. Surrender is not a weakness; it is *divine strength!*[11]

When you think of surrendering, you may envision someone "waving the white flag," a major defeat, a loss. When you surrender to the Holy Spirit, it is quite the opposite; it's not about "giving up" control, it's about *"giving over"* control, *entrusting*; there's a huge difference!

If you are worried about surrender sounding like a "bad thing," it is the exact opposite. You will feel lighter (you're not carrying around all that baggage); you will be more joyful (relieved you are not in charge anymore); you will have a freedom that surpasses all understanding and a wonderful peace you have never before felt. You are now on a path following the Holy Spirit, Jesus...God. You *know* where that will lead you, so you see, you don't lose anything; you gain *everything!*

God has a plan for your life; you know it's a good one because *it's God's plan!* You also have free will to choose "your plan." Oftentimes, it's *not* the best plan.[12] When you surrender to the Holy Spirit, you are saying "God – I am following Your plan, because You truly know what is best for me, and I trust You."

Now, God does not want part of you; He wants all of you.[13] He doesn't want you to trust Him only with your circumstances; God wants you to trust Him with *yourself!* God knows it's not an easy thing to do; that is why you have the Holy Spirit here helping you. He will guide you, empower you, He will warn you, help you pray; the Holy Spirit will lead you to salvation if you follow Him. Isn't it time you gave yourself entirely to Him?

You need to wake up every morning and surrender to His Spirit. Why every day? *Every day* you are faced with "the flesh" that wants to overtake you, in your thoughts, in your words and in your actions.[14]

You have the power over "the flesh" because of The Holy Spirit. "In the flesh" refers to the deeds of a sinner: selfish desires, immorality, jealousy, hatred, anything contrary to the character of Christ. The fruit of the Spirit, or character of Christ is love, joy, peace, patience kindness, goodness, faithfulness, gentleness, and self-control (Galatians 5:22-23 NLT).

> You, my brothers and sisters, were called to be free. But do not use your freedom to indulge the flesh; rather, serve one another humbly in love...
>
> Walk by the Spirit, and you will not gratify the desires of the flesh. For the flesh desires what is contrary to the Spirit, and the Spirit what is contrary to the flesh. They are in conflict with each other, so that you are not to do whatever you want.
>
> **Galatians 5:13,16-17**

When you choose to live by the Spirit, you "put to death" the evil deeds of the body and you will live forever.

> We have an obligation – but it is not to the flesh, to live according to it. For if you live according to the flesh, you will die; but if by the Spirit you put to death the misdeeds of the body, you will live.
>
> **Romans 8:12-13**

When you surrender every day to the Holy Spirit, His strength takes over in you. Personally, during my day, if I am tempted to say or do *(or even think)* something from my "old self," I pause, and I say to myself, "This *must* be the flesh talking because it sure doesn't sound like the Spirit." Then I can overrule the "old self" and let the "new self," the *new* me in Jesus, take over.

The Holy Spirit will begin to change you in ways you never imagined. As your transformation begins, you discover God's plan for yourself. God's plan replaces your random walk through life with a life full of meaning and purpose, life-changing purpose.

Rick Warren writes there are three things that can stand in the way of your surrendering to God: fear, pride, and confusion. Is one or more of these holding you back?[15]

To be honest, what held me back was confusion over what surrender really meant. I had a vision of the white flag waving in the wind, feeling as if I was admitting defeat. Now I realize how foolish I was. All surrendering meant was that I was acknowledging that God, *my Creator*, was in charge of my life. He made me, I belong to Him, and so *He is in charge* – period! And because I love Him with all my heart, I trust Him to do what God the Father needs to do: guide, love and teach me. Any parent would want that responsibility while raising his or her child. *You know* what is in your child's best interest; you instinctively want to protect and nurture your child and prepare him or her for the future. God is doing the same thing, our future being eternity with Him. So once again, the first step in our preparation for eternity is surrendering our lives to God.

There are so many distractions in life competing to be number one: distractions of "the flesh." It is *impossible* for you to fulfill God's personal plan if you place the gathering and accumulation of earthly possessions ahead of Him. When you choose to follow "your plan," you put God second.

While life offers a multitude of choices, it all comes down to only one when your time on this earth is over, and that is where you choose to spend eternity. Make the commitment to choose Jesus today to be the Lord and Savior of your life, and put God first.

Having a daily prayer practice reminds you *every day* that you are to please and honor God in all you do. It's harder to choose to walk "in the flesh" when you are promising God daily to obey and do His Will.

When God is first in your life, and you model your behavior after Christ, you are abundantly blessed in many ways. The Bible reminds you though that *all your blessings*, everything on this earth, belong to God; you have been given the privilege to enjoy God's possessions while you are here, but God says not to get too attached to them because they are all temporary.[16] Instead, you must place emphasis on what you cannot see, which will last forever.

The earth is the Lord's, and everything in it.
The world and all its people belong to him.

**Psalm 24:1 NLT**

The things we see now will soon be gone, but
the things we cannot see will last forever.

**2 Corinthians 4:18 NLT**

God wants you to enjoy life and all it has to offer. He wants you to be generous and share your blessings. God also gives you the responsibility to use them in a way that would please Him.

"For I know the plans I have for you," declares
the Lord, "plans to prosper you and not to harm
you, plans to give you hope and a future."

**Jeremiah 29:11**

Those who are trusted with something valuable
must show they are worthy of that trust.

**1 Corinthians 4:2 NCV**

When you leave this earth, you leave everything behind, everything except for your character; the character you've spent your *entire* life transforming into Christ's likeness.

Do not confuse character with personality. God created you to be unique in whom you are, but He wants you to have *His* values.[17] Remember the fruit of the Spirit, the characteristics of Christ: love, joy, peace, patience, kindness, goodness, faithfulness, gentleness and self-control (Galatians 5:22-23 NLT).

Do not waste one more day; start today to focus on following the plan God has for you. It doesn't matter what your past looks like. You can start over right now! God loves you unconditionally. If you turn away from your past and your sin, no matter what has transpired, Jesus will forgive you. Jesus will direct, strengthen, encourage, and heal you, *and so much more.*

Surrender to the Holy Spirit and invite Him to rule your life. He will take you on the most glorious adventures. Your life will become different in the most amazing, beautiful way. When you are aligned with the Holy Spirit, a magnificent change occurs within you. You will feel the change in your relationship with God, your outlook on life, even your attitude towards yourself and others will change. Your challenges and circumstances will look different! The Holy Spirit will help you look at life through the eyes of love, faith and trust: *through the eyes of Jesus.* You are now standing on Christ's rock, and it is a position of strength, confidence, courage and complete trust.

Trust in the Lord with all your heart and lean not on
your own understanding; in all your ways submit
to him, and he will make your paths straight.

**Proverbs 3:5-6**

## "Daily surrender to the Holy Spirit" Prayer

*Spirit of God, I surrender to You. Show me today how I can
serve the Almighty Father in a mighty way. Fill me with the fruit
of Your Spirit -- love, joy, peace, patience, kindness, goodness,
faithfulness, gentleness, and self-control -- so all my words,
thoughts and actions edify and honor God our Father.*

*Strengthen me with Your power O Holy Spirit, so I may be
successful today in winning the battle between flesh and
Spirit. Please guide me, Holy Spirit, help me to discover God's
Will for my life.*

*In Jesus' Holy name.*

*Amen*

# 5 - PAUSE BEFORE YOU GO

As you strive each day to walk faithfully "in the Spirit" to become more Christ-like in how you live your life, you will need help along the way to be successful.

You may find it helpful to consciously "pause," have a five-second delay so you can align yourself with The Holy Spirit, with Jesus, with God, and *then yourself.*

This "pause" can help you think with the fruit of the Spirit instead of "in the flesh," making a big difference in how you approach life and in the results you obtain. Christ-likeness only happens when you make Christ-like choices. When you change the way you think by thinking "in the Spirit," your life will change. Remember every action begins as a thought.[18]

When are good times to "Pause?"

- Before you give praise to God: reflect on your blessings, an answered prayer, or just to give thanks. Think about what you want to say to God; speak from your heart; speak with sincerity and truth.

- Before you pray each day: remember to acknowledge and give thanks for the good in your life; don't go directly to what's wrong in your life. Think about Jesus and the supreme sacrifice He made for you. What do you want to say to Him?

- As you pray: don't forget to be still and listen for God's response. Remember you want to open a dialogue with Him; embrace His wisdom.

- Before you give into temptation: ask Jesus to help you. He was also tempted; He will give you the strength to resist.

- Before you overreact to an obstacle placed in your path: acknowledge who is responsible (Satan) and react accordingly (chapter 12).

- Before you speak, think, or act "in the flesh:" ask the Holy Spirit to get you back on track and keep you walking "in the Spirit."

- Before you ask for forgiveness: search your heart; Jesus will help you.

- Before you make big decisions: pray to God for wisdom and understanding. Ask the Holy Spirit to give you the right timing.

- Before you answer a tough question: ask the Holy Spirit to help you find the right words to express yourself.

- Before you get into a confrontation: pray to God for wisdom and understanding. Ask the Holy Spirit to help you find the right words to defuse the situation in a kind and gracious way. Ask Him to help you behave in a Christ-like manner.

- If you are already in a conflict: pray to God for wisdom and understanding so you can bring a fair and just resolution to the table. Ask Christ to be the mediator; ask the Holy Spirit to help you speak "in the Spirit."

Set yourself up for success; "pausing" will help you do just that. Take the time necessary to say and do the right thing. You have access to the wisest teachers, counselors, and intercessors: God the Father, God the Son, and God the Holy Spirit. Converse with them; they are waiting to hear from you. They are all waiting to help you.

It is the spirit in a person, the breath of the
Almighty, that gives them understanding.

### Job 32:8

### "The Pause" Prayer

*Dear Almighty God,*

*I pray that I may be fearless in expressing my honesty in all aspects of my life in a kind and gracious way. Help me to break the habits of my old self and to uncover the new self, to be more like Your Son, Jesus Christ.*

*By the power of the Holy Spirit, may old reactions, responses and words be "paused" so that I can infuse them with His love, respect, honesty and humility before releasing them. I ask the Holy Spirit to show me the right way, Your way, Father, so I choose always to walk in the Spirit, choosing Your plan, Your Will for my life.*

*May my trust and faith in You, Dear Father, be strengthened thorough the grace of Your Son, Jesus Christ.*

*I ask all this, according to Your Holy Will.*

*Amen*

# 6 - PRAYER IS A PRIORITY

Why is it important that you pray? Daily prayer will keep you connected to God. Talking with Him and *listening to Him* will heighten your awareness and thankfulness of how He is working in your life. You communicate with God through prayer. Praying is your opportunity to share every part of your life with Him. As life changes, so do your prayers. You share your successes and joy with God; you ask Him for help in times of adversity. You ask God to forgive you through prayer. You strengthen your relationship with God, His beloved Son Jesus, and the Holy Spirit through prayer. You praise God through prayer. Prayer is your lifeline!

My soul, find rest in God; my hope comes from him.

Trust in him at all times, you people; pour out
your hearts to him, for God is our refuge.

**Psalm 62:5,8**

It's amazing how often we neglect the big things that our hearts, souls, spirits, mind and body need the most because of all the little things we cram into our day. Prayer isn't the only thing in our life that suffers; what about sleep, exercise, conversations with loved ones, quality one-on-one time with family and most importantly with God?

It's not always easy to set aside time to pray; what works best for me is spending my coffee time in the morning with my prayer book and my Bible. Start by finding even 10 or 15 minutes in your day (and/or night); it will make a significant difference. Personally, I love starting my day off with gratitude in my heart and God's Word tucked safely inside me. How much nicer it is to start your day with joy, inspiration and hope, rather than worry, fear or doubt!

Pray in the Spirit on all occasions with
all kinds of prayers and requests.

**Ephesians 6:18**

If you slow yourself down and open yourself to hear and receive God's Word, you will be amazed at how much wisdom, love and guidance His Word contains and how relevant it is to your life. *God's Word is alive!* God's Word will add a whole new dimension *that speaks to you.* What you learn may just help you make better decisions and create change in your life.

The Word of God is alive and powerful. It
exposes our innermost thoughts and desires.

**Hebrews 4:12 NLT**

When you read God's Word and write down your prayers, you open up a dialogue with Him. It's no longer a monologue. The hope and encouragement that come from this prayer practice are immense.

God does not want you to talk with Him only during your quiet time; He wants to hear from you throughout your day.[19] As you strive to become closer with the Holy Spirit, ask Him each day to guide you, to give you the right words. Give thanks to God for loving you and for blessing you so abundantly. Talk with Jesus; ask Him to help you resist temptation and thank Him for sacrificing His life to save you. Ask Jesus to help you think as He thinks.

You can do this while you are driving in the car, washing the dishes, standing in line at the food market, working throughout the day, getting the children ready for school in the morning; the point is that you don't want to limit your time with God to a quiet moment at home with little or no distraction. Practice keeping Him in your thoughts through your busy, noisy day; this is another way to show your devotion to Him and to strive to live "in the Spirit," more naturally.

It doesn't happen overnight; routines are hard to change. Pray for the courage and strength to start prioritizing your day by putting God first. With practice and dedication, it will happen. After a while, it will become your new normal, the new you in Jesus. Trust God to help you. Step aside, stop interfering with His work, and *let God lead you!*

> Let the morning bring me word of your unfailing love, for I have put my trust in you. Show me the way I should go, for to you I entrust my life.

**Psalm 143:8**


### "Prioritize my day" Prayer


*Dear Heavenly Father,*

*I ask that You bless me with the strength and wisdom to plan each day around my prayer time with You. Hearing Your Word, Father, adds so much joy and hope to my life. I look forward to asking You for direction and help with concerns that arise. I am so grateful for having the opportunity to worship You in a deep and powerful way.*

*May the grace and strength of Your Son, Jesus Christ be with me, Father, as each day I choose to follow in His footsteps, to honor and glorify You. Praise be to You.*

*Amen*

And lastly, when you pray, believe with all your heart that God hears you. Trust God to keep His promises.

> When you ask, you must believe and not doubt, because the one who doubts is like a wave of the sea, blown and tossed by the wind.

**James 1:6**

# 7 - SPEAK INTO BEING – WORDS ARE POWERFUL

When God created the universe, He said:

> "Let there be light," and there was light.

**Genesis 1:3**

Now listen to what Jesus taught the disciples:

> "Have faith in God," Jesus answered. "Truly I tell you, if anyone says to this mountain, 'Go, throw yourself into the sea,' and does not doubt in their heart but believes that what they say will happen, it will be done for them. Therefore I tell you, whatever you ask for in prayer, believe that you have received it, and it will be yours."

**Mark 11:22–24**

Jesus is teaching *you* to use God's faith and speak it. When you speak into being, you speak *to* the situation, not *about* the situation. Tell the mountain to move; whether a health mountain, a financial mountain, whatever *your* mountain is, speak to it and tell it to *move*.[20] Believe it will be done. That is how you use God's faith and the divine power of the Holy Spirit.

What is your mountain? Health, finances, relationship, business, church, family…Speak to it!

### **"Move my mountain" Prayer**

### (state your mountain's name)

*By the power of God, the Almighty, you are demolished; I am released from your stronghold. You are nothing more than dust beneath my feet. An open door has taken your place, an open door that no man can close. Through the grace and strength of Jesus Christ, I walk through this door, free of this bondage, guided by the Holy Spirit, to love and serve the Lord.*

*I praise God for His mercy and love and give Him all the glory.*

*Amen*

Why are the words you choose so important?

Jesus said:

> "For the mouth speaks what the heart is full of. A good man brings good things out of the good stored up in him, and an evil man brings evil things out of the evil stored up in him."

**Matthew 12:34–35**

To encourage someone is to pour courage into him or her.[21] I just love that. Who doesn't want to do that for those we love? Who doesn't want to do that for anyone, *period!* I would much rather pour courage into those who need it then to criticize or judge. It doesn't cost a thing to say something uplifting to someone.

Encourage one another and build each other up.

**1 Thessalonians 5:11**

When you have an opportunity to lift someone up and fill him or her with hope, courage and strength, you can also help someone break cycles, push the reset button, and "shoot" for the stars. Your inspiration and kindness can change someone's life; *now that's powerful!*

Gracious words are a honeycomb, sweet
to the soul and healing to the bones.

**Proverbs 16:24**

Negative words do nothing to improve the quality of your life. "My feet are killing me." "This job will be the death of me." "That scared me to death." Just as you can choose positive words to "speak into being" your prayers, you can unintentionally choose negative words to "speak into being" sickness, hopelessness, and defeat. Jerry Savelle, author of *If Satan Can't Steal Your Joy…He Can't Keep Your Goods*, writes "Satan has deceitfully, but cleverly, injected death into our vocabulary so that now we use it unconsciously as a manner of expression."[22]

The negative words you use may not affect you immediately. The Bible says it is a process we unconsciously set in motion.[23]

The tongue has the power of life and death

**Proverbs 18:21**

Remember, the words you speak are *your* choice. Try each day to think before you speak; pray for that five-second delay. Choose words wisely that will glorify God and edify the person you are talking to or about, *yourself included!*

The wise in heart are called discerning, and
gracious words promote instruction.

**Proverbs 16:21**

### "May my mouth be filled with kind words" Prayer

*Dearest Holy Spirit,*

*You lovingly guide me each day with Your strength, glory and supreme wisdom. May my mouth be filled with pure loving words and may not an unkind and gossiping word leave my lips. Please fill me with Your goodness and compassion.*

*I strive each day to choose Your words, Your thoughts, and reflect in all my actions, ways in which to edify the Father in a glorious way so I may set a good example to others through my love for You.*

*Thank You for teaching me, Holy Spirit, for guiding me to do the Will of the Holy Father.*

# 8 - STAND IN THE GAP

"Standing in the Gap" means to provide support, to step in, to pray for someone, to be his or her advocate before God. You bring your requests to the Lord for your loved one, or just someone God lays on your heart. You faithfully continue to do so until results are seen. It's not a one-time prayer. You pray with all your heart, offering that person strength and encouragement, and you petition our Heavenly Father on his or her behalf.

> "I looked for someone among them who would build up the wall and stand before me in the gap."
>
> **Ezekiel 22:30**

To help give you a visual of this, think of how God instructed Moses to use his staff to part the Red Sea. Moses was desperately trying to save the Israelites from the Egyptians. They came upon the Red Sea, and Moses lifted his staff and took the first step...Faith! The Holy Spirit, with all of His power and might, did as God requested and created a wind so fierce and strong that it divided the sea. Moses immediately stepped out in faith. He stood in the gap for the Israelites so they could cross the sea. After they safely crossed, God told Moses to lift his staff again; he did and stepped out of the gap. The sea swallowed up all of the Egyptians. Moses demonstrated his faith by acting as an intercessor for the Israelites. Moses had to take the first step though...the step of faith for all who followed. He believed God would show up, and He Did! Praise God!

You can do the same; believe it or not, you have the same power as a child of God. You stand in the gap for those who need God by bringing your requests to Him, asking God to "part the sea" in their lives, making the pathway clear.

We all need a little extra help when times get tough. If someone asks you for prayer, try wrapping a prayer around the circumstances and God's Holy Word, so that together you can pray the same prayer. Ask him or her to tell you when the prayer has been answered, so you can both check off the prayer request and give thanks to God – together! Remember God's ways aren't always our ways, so His answer and timing may be different from what you expect.

Jesus said:

> "Where two or three gather in my
> name, there am I with them."

**Matthew 18:20**

You'll be amazed how present God will be in your life through the practice of praying for others. When you help in carrying your loved one's burden, a feeling of fellowship and responsibility comes with it. You walk in the Spirit more confidently and keep God in the forefront of your mind.

> Carry each other's burdens, and in this
> way you will fulfill the law of Christ.

**Galatians 6:2**

It is important to pray for others; it is important to have someone praying for *you*, to encourage you, to help you, to stand in the gap *for you*. There may be times when you are too weak to pray. It is wonderful when there is someone you can count on to pray for you. Maybe they've asked *you* for prayer. Look for someone who has a relationship with God, who loves and trusts Him and who is a positive force in your life.

Pray for each other so that you may be healed. The prayer of a righteous person is powerful and effective.

**James 5:16**

## <u>"Standing in the Gap" Prayer</u>

*Dear Heavenly Father,*

*I humbly bring my prayer to You. I feel in my heart,*

<u>*(insert name)*</u>

*is suffering. I stand here today to offer hope and encouragement, promising to walk faithfully beside (insert name), lovingly helping to lighten (his/her) burden.*

*I ask the Holy Spirit to guide and comfort (insert name) during this challenging time, and I ask You, Father, to bless (insert name) with the grace and strength of Your Son, Jesus Christ.*

*Praise be to You, Dear Father, for Your divine love for all of Your children.*

*Amen*

# 9 - WHEN OTHERS MAY NOT SHARE THE SAME BELIEFS

We would all like everyone around us to share in the same love, belief and faith in God. Unfortunately, there are those whose hearts aren't open to God's Word. Do not be discouraged. Your prayers will benefit them too. Remember your generational blessings. As much as you want to help others, you cannot change them; only God can change a person's heart, life, or direction. In fact, any transformation you experience in your *own* character is from God, through the grace of our Lord, Jesus Christ, and by the power of the Holy Spirit.

You can set a good example in all you do: in your words, in how you talk about God, pray before meals, exchange kind words with one another, and model Jesus' life through your actions.

Jesus said:

> "Let your light shine before others, that they may see your good deeds and glorify your Father in heaven."

**Matthew 5:16**

You can stand in the gap for those who lack a relationship with God, especially when they directly influence you and your family. Their words and actions reflect their need for God; they just don't know how to let Him in...*yet!* Instead of trying to change, judge or condemn them, lend support through prayer. Ask God to open the eyes of their hearts so they can receive Him and His Word. Pray for them. If you have the opportunity, pour words of encouragement into them.

"Even sinners will be rescued; they will be
rescued because your hands are pure."

**Job 22:30 NLT**

### "May my faith set an example" Prayer

*Dear God,*

*May Your Holy Spirit guide me, so that I can set an example
for those around me. Soften their hearts and minds to hear the
gospel truth about love, forgiveness and redemption. Help me to
deliver a clear, simple way for them to grasp Your magnificent
love. May the faith and Word that live in my heart find a direct
path to their hearts and fill them with hope and inspiration for
You, Almighty Father.*

*Amen*

Make a difference today! Don't let *anyone* you know and love reach
a point in their lives when they need God but don't know how to
ask Him for help because they don't have a relationship with Him.
Encourage, teach, demonstrate and lead by example in showing how
powerful prayer is.

How can we expect our children and our children's children to sow
seeds for their families if they don't know how? I pray the eyes of
all hearts, in your family's and mine, open wide to receive and share
God's love.

The only thing that counts is faith
expressing itself through love.

**Galatians 5:6**

God's people are everywhere. You are probably surrounded by them, but not always aware. Do they acknowledge God? Do people you know outwardly thank and praise Him? Do they appear comfortable about sharing their thoughts about God?

I pray you are fearless about expressing your faith, but if you're like I was, pray for strength and confidence. Acknowledge God; give Him credit when life goes amazingly well, or when you witness something breathtakingly beautiful; offer your support to others through prayer and share your story of how God makes a difference in your life.

Once in a while, when I share how God and prayer changed my life, someone will say to me they are "not religious." I'm pretty sure this is their way of saying, "thanks, but no thanks," as if I am selling something. I remind them that for me, it's not so much about religion; it's the *relationship* with God that's important.

Some people have had bad experiences or have preconceived ideas about religious institutions, clergy, etc. which may contribute to why they are not comfortable talking about God. I am sure many have valid reasons to feel this way; perhaps they even blame God. I am not qualified to help them overcome their feelings, but God is. I always try and encourage those who have hardened hearts to consider going to God and talking to Him about their concerns, to listen to what He has to say, and to make peace with Him. All we can do is plant the seed, pray for them, and set an example for them, living a life that reflects Christ within us.

In order for us to do the Will of our Father, we cannot deny God. If the Word of God lives in you, share it! Plant a seed; let the world around you know. You just never know when your expression of faith will help someone be released from fear, or unexplainably change their life. It may be someone in your family. Show your faith in God; be brave and praise His name.

The Spirit God gave us does not make us timid,
but gives us power, love and self-discipline. Do not
be ashamed of the testimony about our Lord.

**2 Timothy 1:7-8**

If you need confidence and courage to openly acknowledge God and praise His name, pray for strength.

### "I fearlessly express my faith" Prayer

*Dear Almighty Father,*

*Grant me supreme strength, wisdom and understanding, so that I may be fearless in expressing my faith.*

*May the power of the Holy Spirit fill me in a mighty way so I can accomplish Your Will, Dear Lord. May He give me the right timing and the perfect words to enlighten those who are placed in my path, sharing with them that Jesus Christ is the Son of God, that through His death and resurrection we are made righteous through faith in Him, and that no one comes to the Father, except through Your Son, Jesus Christ.*

*I honor and worship You Dearest Father and give You all the glory, honor and praise this day and every day following.*

*Amen*

# 10 - FORGIVE YOURSELF

When I humbly bring to God my sins with a sincere heart of regret, and ask Him for His forgiveness, I know He forgives me. When I apologize to someone and ask for forgiveness, and it is given it to me; I know in my heart I've been forgiven.

What is the most difficult part of forgiveness? It is forgiving *ourselves* and letting the past be the past. We all make mistakes. At times, we choose the wrong path. No one is perfect. Only Jesus was perfect in sin and death.

If you are having trouble forgiving yourself or if there is something from your past that keeps you from moving forward, this little exercise may help you. Visualize yourself pulling out a piece of luggage from the closet. Open the lid. Gather all your sins, regrets, hurts, and one at a time lay them all out on the bed. Acknowledge each one. Ask God to forgive you for each sin. Then fold them up neatly and place them in the suitcase, one by one. Say goodbye as if they are going on a journey from which they will never return. Once your suitcase is packed, pick it up and take it to the cross, to Calvary. If this is your first time, ask the Holy Spirit to reveal His light and show you the way.

When you get there, Jesus will be waiting. Lay the suitcase at the foot of the cross and look up at Him. Ask Him for forgiveness; tell Him you are so sorry for all the mistakes made in your life. Say, "Lord, help me." He will lovingly receive all of your "baggage" and the Almighty Father will immediately forgive *all* of your sins.

God knows your weakness; He made you. Your inability to forgive yourself would be your cross to bear, so God left you a gift at the foot of the cross from the Holy Spirit. Pick it up when you drop off your "old self." Take it home with you, and when you open it, you will find your redemption. Gone is the past, completely gone in God's eyes. He forgives and forgets! You are forgiven for everything. Even if you forgot to pack a small sin, a recurring sin – Jesus knows; He sees your heart and wants you free: free from sin, free from guilt! You get a new start – so go ahead and push the reset button on your life; you get to start "anew." You are a new person in Christ Jesus!

Sometimes it takes more than one trip to the cross. If you have a hidden sin, the Lord will reveal it to you. Ask Him, "Lord, what do I do that breaks your heart? Break mine with what breaks Yours." Leave it all at the cross. Push the reset button; start over. Jesus is waiting to help; the Almighty Father is waiting to receive you...to forgive you.

Jesus died on the cross to save you from your sins, a just man dying for the unjust. He rose from the dead so that you are made righteous through your faith in Him. Do not let Calvary and Christ's death be in vain. The Lord forgives you. What else could you possibly need?

In him we have redemption through his
blood, the forgiveness of sins, in accordance
with the riches of God's grace.

**Ephesians 1:7**

### "I receive Your redemption" Prayer

*Dear Heavenly Father,*

*I thank You for Your divine love; love so deep, so abundant, it washes away my sins. I embrace the redemption You have blessed me with, through the supreme sacrifice of Your beloved Son, Jesus Christ.*

*As I walk forward in life as a new person in Christ, my eyes are fixed on following the Holy Spirit. As He guides me on my path, I continue to pray for strength and courage so that each day my steps are in line with the Spirit, and so that one day I may be worthy of spending eternity with You. I sing Your praises, today and every day of my life.*

*Amen*

# 11 - THE ARMOR OF GOD

**Stand in the power of the blood of Christ. Read the Armor of God and make it part of your daily prayer practice:**

Be strong in the Lord and in his mighty power.

Put on the full armor of God, so that you can take your stand against the devil's schemes.

For our struggle is not against flesh and blood, but against the rulers, against the authorities, against the powers of this dark world and against the spiritual forces of evil in the heavenly realms.

Therefore put on the full armor of God, so that when the day of evil comes, you may be able to stand your ground, and after you have done everything, to stand.

Stand firm then, with the belt of truth buckled around your waist, with the breastplate of righteousness in place, and with your feet fitted with the readiness that comes from the gospel of peace.

In addition to all this, take up the shield of faith, with which you can extinguish all the flaming arrows of the evil one.

Take the helmet of salvation and the sword of the Spirit, which is the word of God.

And pray in the Spirit on all occasions with all kinds of prayers and requests. With this in mind, be alert and always keep on praying for all of the Lord's people.

**Ephesians 6:10-18**

The Armor of God gives you the tools you need in order to be victorious over all temptations:[24]

- **Belt of Truth:** It wraps around you and holds you up; the Armor of God helps you to be able to tell the difference between truth and deception.

- **Breast Plate of Righteousness:** It covers and guards your heart; it is the righteousness of Christ.

- **Gospel of Peace:** Shoes of peace; you can walk in all His ways; prepares your feet for warfare; brings with you the message of grace.

- **Shield of Faith:** Hold it up against all attacks; protects you from Satan's attempt to plant doubt in your mind and heart.

- **The Helmet of Salvation:** Covers and protects your head, enables you to tell the difference between truth and deception and resist temptation.

- **The Sword of the Spirit - The Word of God:** Sharper than any double-edged sword. Speak God's Word and watch it cut through all negativity and attacks; your offensive weapon in overpowering Satan.

- **Pray in the Spirit:** Through prayer, God gives you spiritual strength; the strength that you need to overcome temptations and all negative circumstances.

# 12 - OVERCOME THE OPPOSITION

Reading God's Word brings you closer to Him and strengthens your faith, trust and hope. God's Word makes sense of life's challenges and gives you the tools to resist "the opposition."

Obviously, the opposition I am referring to is Satan. I know that's a pretty scary word, but I'm a firm believer that knowledge is power. I'm not going to hide my head in the sand and pretend he doesn't exist. If you believe in good, you must believe in evil. Evil is very real. Knowing who the opposition is and how he works is important. Even more important is your knowledge that through Jesus and His supreme sacrifice, *you* have the power and authority over the opposition.

> The weapons we fight with are not the weapons
> of the world. On the contrary, they have
> divine power to demolish strongholds.

### 2 Corinthians 10:4

We should all be prepared, defeating Satan before he entices us, leads us astray, or casts doubt on our situation or circumstance. Satan is notorious for trying to steal happiness and plant doubt in our minds. Every time a crisis arises, Satan has an opportunity to take from you, *including God's Word* from your heart. This is when your faith is tested. The main tool of protection is using the Word of God to fight Satan. Rick Warren writes, "There is power in God's Word, and Satan fears it." He also goes on to say, "...memorizing Scripture is absolutely essential to defeating temptation," another important reason to include God's Word with your prayers! As you make Scripture part of your everyday prayer practice, God's Word will become firmly rooted in your heart, and it will be ready at a moment's notice to help you stand up against the enemy.[25]

Another important tool is the Armor of God. Begin your day by dressing appropriately – putting on *all* of God's protection. Read it first thing in the morning, before you check emails, take a phone call, read the paper, and before you discuss anything of importance.

Who is the opposition? A fallen angel who is out to steal, rob and destroy.

Lucifer, whose name means "Morning Star," was the perfect angel. The sin that corrupted him was self-generated pride. Lucifer assumed that he was equal to, if not better than God. Lucifer was cast out of heaven along with his followers; his name changed to Satan, meaning "Adversary." **This was when Satan's warfare against the work of God through mankind began, and it still continues!**

Look at what surrounds us in the world today: greed, sinfulness, hate, crime, destruction and cruelty to humanity. It is all Satan's work, and from the magnitude of it, it is evident that Satan's way is the easy way. It takes no effort to do the wrong thing, to disregard and disobey rules, whereas it takes strength of character and courage to do the right thing. Satan uses his limited ability to test believers in order to "sift" through them, to see who truly is a believer. Those who hold fast and resist temptation are kept in faith through the advocacy of Christ.

> Submit yourselves, then, to God. Resist
> the devil, and he will flee from you.

**James 4:7**

Although Satan's *only* weapon is deception, do not underestimate him; he is a master at it. He has to be. It's his only hope of keeping you from following God.

He works in your life trying to fill you with doubt, anger, intimidation and fear. Let's not forget about temptation and all those nasty obstacles he puts in your way to frustrate you.

Satan will exploit your weaknesses. You may not even be consciously aware of those areas, *but he is.* He knows your triggers, where you are vulnerable; he looks for old or recently healed emotional wounds.[26] The question is not "What will you do *if* you are tempted?" but "*When* you are tempted, what will you do?"

"Watch and pray so that you will not fall into temptation. The spirit is willing, but the flesh is weak."

**Matthew 26:41**

Satan also loves to try and get you to speak in a negative way. He knows that the words of "death" and "fear" are toxic. It is another way he can try to steal God's Word from you and attempt to destroy you. **If you fill your heart with God's Word and meditate daily on them, then what you have in your heart will come out of your mouth.**[27]

I have hidden your word in my heart
that I might not sin against you.

**Psalm 119:11**

Satan can interfere with forgiving yourself or can make you feel unworthy of forgiveness. This is his attempt to hold you back and make you feel powerless. Remember that you have an all-forgiving Father who is merciful and compassionate.

Satan will try anything to defeat you: lies, distractions, mixed truth, discouragement. He will drag up your past failures or those of a loved one, even go as far as bringing sickness, sorrow and poverty.

Remember that God loves His children supremely, and although Satan is a frightening force, God never leaves you without options to overcome him. This is why Jesus died on the cross for your sins. You have the victory; Jesus paid the price. Do not let Jesus' sacrifice be in vain.

God is faithful; he will not let you be tempted beyond
what you can bear. But when you are tempted, he will
also provide a way out so that you can endure it.

### 1 Corinthians 10:13

It is important to know that temptation not only gives you the
opportunity to do the wrong thing, it gives you the opportunity to do
the *right thing!* Every time you resist temptation, you further develop
and strengthen your character to be in the image of Jesus Christ.[28]
And that is a beautiful thing!

From my personal experience, Satan's "work" comes in different
forms and in many levels of intensity. Sometimes he can be so subtle,
planting just a seed or two of doubt or guilt in your mind. It can be
difficult at first to know for certain if it is Satan's work or not; he's that
good at what he does. It's as if Satan purposely flies "under the radar"
at times, hoping to go unnoticed. He is counting on you to finish the
job he starts, hoping you will dwell on the negativity he just planted
until you are feeling really bad about yourself.

Now is when you need to "pause" and align yourself with the Spirit.
Look at your situation; if it is not reflective of the fruit of the Spirit --
love, joy, peace, patience, kindness, goodness, faithfulness, gentleness
and self-control -- you can rest assured it is the work of Satan.

Next time Satan plants seeds of doubt in your mind stand up and say:

**Satan, you have no authority over me. You are defenseless, for the
grace and strength of our Lord Jesus Christ is within *me,* and *I*
have the power over *you,* and your deeds!**

Once you make this statement, you must shift your focus to something
else *immediately!* The more you try and resist the temptation the more
you think about it; keeping it alive, engaging in battle with it. Do not
water the seeds Satan planted. Refocus and move on.[29]

There are days when an incident will frustrate or anger you (you lost or broke something, your plan didn't go as expected, money had to be spent for a repair, you just washed your red sweatshirt with the whites – the list is long!); you can be confident it is Satan trying to ruin your day. Every time he succeeds in frustrating you, it's a win for him.

He will *very* patiently chip away at your confidence, sanity and happiness. Next time something like this happens, try saying, "Hmmm...that's interesting..." This may sound a bit silly, but it works. Somehow this little phrase disrupts your instinctive reaction of getting upset, angry, or frustrated. It's a mini "time-out and regroup" exercise. Once you identify the source of trouble (the "opposition"), immediately focus your energy on fixing what happened _calmly._ Do not let Satan win! He knows if he can make you unhappy or angry, you can't be a joyful believer.[30]

It's not easy to pretend that what just happened doesn't bother you; it takes focus, effort and practice. By bravely dealing with the situation in a positive way, you beat him at his own game. You will no longer blame yourself, or anyone else for that matter, for what has happened, thus removing the former guilt, frustration or anger. Don't give him the satisfaction of winning.

There will be times when a true crisis presents itself. First, pray to God and then place a call to someone who can immediately pray with you, pray *for* you, stand in the gap for you. Prayer will give you the strength and courage to overcome any situation. Don't forget there is power in numbers. For every way that Satan tries to defeat you, there is a way to beat him. No questions about it, you have God on your side.

> The God of peace will soon crush Satan under your
> feet. The grace of our Lord Jesus be with you.

**Romans 16:20**

## "Protect me from Satan" Prayer

*Dear Jesus,*

*My Lord and great Redeemer, I ask the Father, in Your Holy name, to protect me from Satan and his followers. When You died for my salvation, You left me the gift of the Holy Spirit to guide and watch over me. May the Holy Spirit fill me with joy and peace and strengthen me with supernatural wisdom to resist and overcome Satan's temptations. I praise God the Father and give Him all the glory.*

*Amen*

Every now and then, Satan may actually be successful in stealing from you. When you lose something – a job, money, you fill in the blank – tell God exactly what has been done and acknowledge that Satan was the attacker. Remember, it is Satan who has set out to make you miserable and have you doubt God. If you stand strong on God's Word with confidence, faith and trust, you can ask God to restore to you sevenfold all you lost. Ask Him to deliver on His promises to scatter the enemy and thank Him for returning sevenfold what was taken.[31]

> The Lord will grant that the enemies who rise up against you will be defeated before you. They will come at you from one direction but flee from you in seven.

> **Deuteronomy 28:7**

> If he is caught, he must pay sevenfold, though it costs him all the wealth of his house.

> **Proverbs 6:31**

### "Return what Satan has stolen" Prayer

*Dear Father,*

*I come to You humbly and ask for Your help. Satan has:*

### *(Describe what has happened to you)*

*I ask You to bless me, Almighty Father, with immense courage and strength. Please deliver me from my troubles. Grant me protection from Satan through the grace of Your Son, Jesus Christ, and scatter Satan and the wickedness that he has brought upon me. I ask You Lord, to deliver on Your promise to return to me sevenfold the:*

### *(Fill in what he stole)*

*I have lost. I ask You this in Your beloved Son's name, Jesus Christ. I praise and glorify You, Father God.*

*Amen*

I hope these suggestions help you recognize and successfully fight off the opposition's attempts to steer you away from God. Pray to God for courage and believe that the power and strength lie within you to fight Satan's wickedness through the grace and love of Jesus Christ and by the power of the Holy Spirit. **Remember, *you* are the lion, not Satan!**[32]

# PART II - CONVERSATIONS WITH GOD - YOUR DAILY PRAYER BOOK

In this section of *PRAYER MADE SIMPLE*, you will find the Daily Prayer Book that contains Scriptures and prayers for different life situations. Here is where you begin your conversations with God. Wrap a prayer around God's Word and make it personal! I believe in my heart that God is waiting to hear all of your prayers.

# HOW TO USE YOUR DAILY PRAYER BOOK

Prayer is an excellent way to start your day, with God's inspiration, hope, and guidance. When you have a daily prayer practice, you strengthen your relationship with God each and every day by taking the time to listen to God and hearing what His plans are for you. Hearing God's Word always adds hope, light and direction to your day.

Find a space, a corner, where your Bible sits; a book to write your prayers; this book; your music; a pad of paper for writing down what comes to your mind while you are praying. If you set it up, then every day you will look at it as if God is asking, "When are you coming? When can we have our time together?" He will be waiting for you and that's a good thing!

Until you feel comfortable with writing your own prayers, I hope this book can help you. Use it for inspiration and to build confidence, so ultimately you will look for Scriptures on your own and write your own prayers. May you open a dialogue with God, read your Bible and let *your* prayer life grow into wonderful conversations with God Almighty.

> Let love and faithfulness never leave
> you; bind them around your neck, write
> them on the tablet of your heart.

**Proverbs 3:3**

Pray, pause and reflect. Is there a special intention for someone in your life? Has someone asked you for prayer? Is there someone in your life who needs prayer for health, finances, employment or some other reason? Perhaps someone close to you needs prayer to invite God into his or her life? What is heavy on *your* heart? Are you facing any challenges? Is there a weakness you would like to strengthen? Every prayer practice should include prayers of gratitude and praise to our Almighty Father. Let God know how thankful you are for blessings already received. Give thanks for an answered prayer, or just be thankful for who God is.

"Write in a book all the words I have spoken to you."

**Jeremiah 30:2**

There are many ways to use this prayer book. You can select a chapter based on your needs or the needs of a loved one. You can read through the chapters until a particular Scripture and prayer spark something inside of you, helping you to pray in ways you normally wouldn't think of, or of whom you normally wouldn't think. It's nice to keep your prayer time fresh and new. Personalize the prayers to include names, specific requests, or circumstances; as your prayers change, just change the wording.

As you begin your conversations with God, hear His message in the Scriptures you read and how they speak to you personally. Meditate on one or more of the passages and then read or say your prayer. This is how you "wrap" your prayer around God's Word! Most important of all, don't over-think the process. You want to look forward to praying, not worry about whether you are doing it right.

I always ask the Holy Spirit to help me pray; perhaps you can too. Ask Him to be with you and guide you as you pray; ask Him who needs prayer. The Holy Spirit loves being in fellowship with you; He loves being close to you.

Remember, the prayers in this book are to get you started, to ignite something within you. Use them however you feel led; there is no right or wrong way.

When you are ready to write your own prayers and find Scripture on your own, check out the back of your Bible where there is a "Concordance" that helps you locate Bible verses that relate to different situations or concerns. If you don't own a Bible, think about purchasing the NIV (New International Version) translation of the Bible. It's extremely easy to understand.

One great resource I have found is an application I use on my iPhone called Bible Gateway. The "app" makes it easy to have the Bible with you at all times. You can read or listen to the Bible in numerous translations, start a Bible reading plan, search for Scripture using keywords such as courage, strength, patience; whatever you need – God's Word has it. The "app" is remarkable! Finding Scripture that "speaks to you" is like finding little treasures.

I sincerely hope you are inspired to reach out to God in all areas of your life, from the smallest to the largest. God's help is a prayer away. Ask, and He will hear. Believe in your heart what you cannot see. Be blessed with the knowledge that God loves you unconditionally. When we ask the Holy Spirit to lead us and we follow with all our heart, our outlook on life, our circumstances and challenges will change *immensely*; just wait and see!

> May he give you the desire of your heart
> and make all your plans succeed.

**Psalm 20:4**

# REJOICE IN THE LORD

# REJOICE IN THE LORD

I will praise the Lord all my life; I will sing
praise to my God as long as I live.

**Psalm 146:2**

The Holy Spirit produces this kind of fruit in our
lives: love, joy, peace, patience, kindness, goodness,
faithfulness, gentleness, and self-control.

**Galatians 5:22–23 NLT**

I will praise God's name in song and
glorify him with thanksgiving.

**Psalm 69:30**

I praise You, God for answering my prayer!

(Reflect on your answered prayer)

I am eternally grateful to be so blessed by Your unconditional love.

I lay my praise at Your feet. I ask You to bless me with all the fruit of Your Spirit – love, joy, peace, patience, kindness, goodness, faithfulness, gentleness, and self-control – so that I may serve You better and those You place in my path.

In Jesus' Holy name, I rejoice in You, Dear Father. I sing Your praise every day of my life.

Amen

# REJOICE IN THE LORD

I will rejoice in the Lord, I will be joyful in God my Savior.

**Habakkuk 3:18**

Sing to the Lord, all the earth; proclaim his salvation
day after day. Declare his glory among the nations,
his marvelous deeds among all peoples.

**1 Chronicles 16:23-24**

O God, we give glory to you all day long
and constantly praise your name.

**Psalm 44:8 NLT**

Dearest Jesus,

What wondrous love You show me despite all of my mistakes and
stumbles. Please forgive me; help me back up on my feet and continue
to shine Your glorious light, illuminating my path.

(Reflect on what you are thankful for and listen for His response)

I continue to pray to be strong and to follow You, Dearest Jesus,
placing each foot carefully one after the other, striving every day to
grow in Your likeness. May my life here on earth prepare me to be
worthy of sharing eternity with You and God our Father.

Amen

# REJOICE IN THE LORD

Always giving thanks to God the Father for
everything, in the name of our Lord, Jesus Christ.

**Ephesians 5:20**

Praise the Lord. How good it is to sing praises to
our God, how pleasant and fitting to praise him!

**Psalm 147:1**

We praise God for the glorious grace
he has poured out on us.

**Ephesians 1:2 NLT**

Father,

By Your amazing love and grace, I stand before You today, grateful for the countless blessings You have bestowed on me.

(Reflect on your blessings and listen for His response)

You have a beautiful plan for me Dear Father. I ask You to continue to fill me with the light, strength and wisdom of the Holy Spirit, so I may live a life worthy of eternal life with You.

May Your glory continue to fill my soul and guide me with a joyful heart.

I rejoice in You Dearest Father; I sing Your praise all day long.

Amen

# REJOICE IN THE LORD

Give thanks to the Lord, for he is
good; his love endures forever.

**1 Chronicles 16:34**

I will give thanks to the Lord because of
his righteousness; I will sing the praises
of the name of the Lord Most High.

**Psalm 7:17**

"O our God, we thank you and
praise your glorious name!"

**1 Chronicles 29:13 NLT**

Thank You, sweet Jesus, for taking my prayer for (yourself or a loved one's name) to the Holy Father. I praise You for so lovingly carrying (my/their) burden and blessing (me/them) with courage and perseverance during this challenging time.

(Reflect on your answered prayer and listen for His response)

Christ Jesus, You send hopelessness away and restore peace to (my/their) life.

I rejoice and give God our Father all the glory, in Your Holy name.

Amen

# PRAYERS FOR EVERY DAY

# PRAYERS FOR EVERY DAY

"For I know the plans I have for you," declares
the Lord, "plans to prosper you and not to harm
you, plans to give you hope and a future."

**Jeremiah 29:11**

What he opens no one can shut, and what he shuts
no one can open. I know your deeds. See, I have
placed before you an open door that no one can
shut. I know that you have little strength, yet you
have kept my word and have not denied my name.

**Revelation 3:7-8**

## Praying for myself

Dearest God,

I ask You to close this chapter of my life:

(Be specific. What is the past, so you can look forward?)

Please open a door that no man can close, a beautiful door that brings
with it a brand new start. Please set my spirit free and deliver me
from all those issues: life's trials and tribulations that try to hold me
back and hurt me.

Bless me with endurance, strength, courage and a peace that surpasses
all understanding. I lift my hands up to You, Heavenly Father and
give You all the glory. I praise and worship You.

Amen

# PRAYERS FOR EVERY DAY

"I tell you, whatever you ask for in prayer, believe that you have received it, and it will be yours."

**Mark 11:24**

"I will do whatever you ask in my name, so that the Father may be glorified in the Son. You may ask me for anything in my name, and I will do it."

**John 14:13-14**

## Praying for myself

Almighty Father,

I call on You to hear my prayer(s):

(Be specific, what is on your heart?)

Strengthen my faith; bless me with abundant patience, for I know in Your perfect timing, I will receive a perfect answer to my prayer. Your ways are not our ways. Even though Your answer may look different from what I expect, I have faith and confidence it will be the best answer for me, for You always have my best interest at heart.

I give You all the glory, Dearest Father. I am grateful for this opportunity to strengthen my character to become more like Your beloved Son, Jesus Christ.

Amen

# PRAYERS FOR EVERY DAY

"Truly I tell you that if two of you on earth agree
about anything they ask for, it will be done for
them by my Father in heaven. For where two or
three gather in my name, there am I with them."

**Matthew 18:19-20**

May he give you the desire of your heart
and make all your plans succeed.

**Psalm 20:4**

## Praying for others

Dearest Jesus,

Please take to Your Father my prayer for (insert names). I pray:

(insert your specific intentions)

Lord and Savior, bless them with immense strength and courage.
Fill them with the confidence to approach and worship God, our
Father, in a powerful and deep way. I pray that (insert names) hear
God's voice, God's truth, and accept His perfect direction. May their
journey through life produce much love, understanding, perseverance
and supreme faith.

All for You, Jesus. Praise be to God.

Amen

# PRAYERS FOR EVERY DAY

This is the confidence we have in approaching God: that
if we ask anything according to his will, he hears us.

**1 John 5:14**

My God will meet all your needs according to
the riches of his glory in Christ Jesus.

**Philippians 4:19**

## Praying for others

I pray to You today Dear God, for (insert names). My prayer is:

(insert your specific intentions)

Please fill them with patience and may they feel firmly rooted in Your love, trusting that their prayer will be answered.

Strengthen (insert names) during this challenging time and help them to have immense hope and faith. May their love for You deepen, their gratitude overflow.

I praise and worship You, Heavenly Father and ask You this in Christ's Holy name.

Amen

# PRAYERS FOR EVERY DAY

Above all else, guard your heart, for
everything you do flows from it.

**Proverbs 4:23**

"This is the meaning of the parable: The seed is the
word of God. But the seed on good soil stands for
those with a noble and good heart, who hear the
word, retain it, and by persevering produce a crop."

**Luke 8:11,15**

## Praying for myself

Father,

I rejoice in Your name, Dear Lord. May joy and happiness fill my
heart, mind and spirit. Fill me with Your wisdom and guidance so
that each day I can fulfill the plan You have set out before me. My
eyes, ears and heart are open and ready to receive Your Word, Your
truth, Your light, Your direction.

### (Be still and listen for His response)

God's grace and glory rises up within me in a wonderful way, and I
sing Your praises. Praise be to God!

Amen

# PRAYERS FOR EVERY DAY

For the Lord is good and his love endures forever;
his faithfulness continues through all generations.

**Psalm 100:5**

I pray that the eyes of your heart may be
enlightened in order that you may know the
hope to which he has called you, the riches of his
glorious inheritance in his holy people, and his
incomparably great power for us who believe.

**Ephesians 1:18-19**

## Praying for myself and all others

Blessed Father, in Your Son, Jesus Christ's name, with grace and strength I approach You and pray for:

(insert names - include yourself and others)

May the eyes of our hearts be enlightened in order that we may know the hope to which You have called us.

Fill us with the knowledge of Your love through all spiritual wisdom and understanding, so that we may become more like Your beloved Son, Jesus Christ.

Bless us with the joy and wisdom of the Holy Spirit. May He carry us along in our journey here in our earthly home until the day we meet You in heaven. Lord consider us worthy.

I ask You all this, according to Your Holy Will.

Amen

# PRAYERS FOR EVERY DAY

I pray that out of his glorious riches he may strengthen you with power through his Spirit in your inner being, so that Christ may dwell in your hearts through faith.

**Ephesians 3:16-17**

Being strengthened with all power according to his glorious might so that you may have great endurance and patience, and giving joyful thanks to the Father, who has qualified you to share in the inheritance of his holy people in the kingdom of light.

**Colossians 1:11-12**

For as the soil makes the sprout come up and a garden causes seeds to grow, so the Sovereign Lord will make righteousness and praise spring up before all nations.

**Isaiah 61:11**

"Ask and it will be given to you; seek and you will find; knock and the door will be opened to you. For everyone who asks receives; the one who seeks finds; and to the one who knocks, the door will be opened."

**Matthew 7:7-8**

# PRAYERS FOR EVERY DAY

## Praying for my family

Dearest Father,

Bless my beautiful family with enormous strength and courage. May they feel Your presence and hold You dearly in their hearts as children of God. May they be like precious seeds, placed lovingly in Your magnificent garden, growing abundantly in faith, joy, hope and love.

May they be fearless in times of adversity, trusting confidently in Your wondrous love, understanding that their pain or suffering is temporary and that You walk through the pain with them and carry them. Teach them to ask the question, "What do You want me to learn?" instead of "Why me?"

May they come to know Your Son, Jesus Christ, and understand the great sacrifice You made in sending us Your only Son. May they walk with Him in their journey through life, drawing on Him for strength. May they learn that the way to be closer to You, Dearest Father, is through Your most precious Son, Jesus Christ, our Savior, our Redeemer.

May they acknowledge the Holy Spirit that dwells within them: calling on Him to direct, guide and help them pray; loving Him tenderly. Please guide them, Dear Lord; show them, help them in knowing all of You.

I ask this according to Your most Holy Will. I honor and worship You, Heavenly Father, and I give You all the glory, all the days of my life. In Jesus' Holy name.

Amen

# FAITH AND TRUST

# FAITH AND TRUST

"If you have faith as small as a mustard seed,
you can say to this mulberry tree, 'Be uprooted
and planted in the sea,' and it will obey you."

**Luke 17:6**

Then Jesus told him, "Because you have seen
me, you have believed; blessed are those who
have not seen and yet have believed."

**John 20:29**

## Praying for myself

Dearest Father,

I strive each day to demonstrate my faith to You and in Your Word. I know faith, even as small as the size of a mustard seed, contains enough power to accomplish what seems impossible: to move mountains. It is not the amount of faith that my heart holds, it's the purity of my faith; no doubt, no unbelief.

May the grace and joy of the Holy Spirit fill me and pour through me with love, knowledge, joy and encouragement for those whose hearts I can reach to share Your Word.

I trust in You Dear Father and hold You close in my heart.

Amen

# FAITH AND TRUST

In you, Lord my God, I put my trust. Show me
your ways, Lord, teach me your paths.

**Psalm 25:1,4**

I have chosen the way of faithfulness; I
have set my heart on your laws.

**Psalm 119:30**

## Praying for myself

Dear Lord,

Your Word lives in my heart. It has made itself at home in me, and I
will care for it, protect it, and share it.

Help me to break the habits of my old self and to uncover my new
self. May old reactions, responses, words and feelings be "paused"
through Your divine grace so that I may infuse them with love,
respect, and humility before releasing them. My goal each and every
day is to become the person that You want me to be; demonstrating
pure faith in all I do.

I thank You for taking me by the hand and leading me. My joy is Your
Word; Your Word is my light, in which I trust.

Amen

# FAITH AND TRUST

Let the morning bring the word of your unfailing love, for I have put my trust in you. Show me the way I should go, for to you I entrust my life.

**Psalm 143:8**

Let us come boldly to the throne of our gracious God. There we will receive his mercy, and we will find grace to help us when we need it most.

**Hebrews 4:16 NLT**

## Praying for others

Dear Father,

Strengthen (insert names), both in faith and in body. May they know that every second of every moment of their life has its value. You are working in them, giving them this time on earth to build and strengthen their character to be in Your Son's likeness. May the eyes of their heart be open to seeing that the only way to You, Almighty King is through Your Son, Jesus Christ.

May their faith in You be abundant, their trust unshakable, remembering that life is all about love.

I ask all this according to Your most Holy Will.

Amen

# FAITH AND TRUST

We wait in hope for the Lord; he is our
help and our shield. In him our hearts
rejoice, for we trust in his holy name.

**Psalm 33:20-21**

Trust in the Lord with all your heart and lean not on
your own understanding; in all your ways submit
to him, and he will make your paths straight.

**Proverbs 3:5-6**

"Blessed is the one who trusts in the
Lord, whose confidence is in him."

**Jeremiah 17:7**

## Praying for others

Dear Lord,

My prayer today is for (insert names). May their faith and trust in You
be strengthened in an amazing way. I pray they embrace the blessing
of Your unconditional, eternal love. May they find solace in Your arms.

Please open (insert names) hearts to receive You fully. Surround
them with Your glory, help guide them in their journey through life.
May they trust in You with all their heart. Lord, may all their paths
be made straight according to Your perfect Will.

Praise be to God.

Amen

# JOY

# JOY

"For the joy of the Lord is your strength."

**Nehemiah 8:10**

Shout for joy to the Lord, all the earth. Worship the Lord
with gladness; come before him with joyful songs.

**Psalm 100:1-2**

The way of the righteous is like the first gleam of dawn,
which shines ever brighter until the full light of day.

**Proverbs 4:18 NLT**

## Praying for myself

Dear Almighty Father,

I rejoice; I am glad; my joy overflows. I strive to be patient. With
You at my side, I will persevere under all circumstances that come
my way. I will keep Your Word safe in my heart and my eyes fixed
on You.

I choose to live my life in all ways to honor and glorify You. May the
Holy Spirit guide my footsteps.

(Be still and listen for His response)

Blessed be God, for the Lord our God is good.

Amen

# JOY

We write this to make our joy complete.

**1 John 1:4**

May the righteous be glad and rejoice before
God; may they be happy and joyful.

**Psalm 68:3**

## Praying for myself

My Lord, my God,

With open eyes and open heart, I joyfully look at all of the blessings
You have so graciously given me; I humbly and openly thank You.

### (Reflect on your blessings)

Father God, Your Word continues to fill me with hope, light and
direction. I joyfully embrace all of You as You guide me through this
magnificent life that You have so lovingly given me.

### (Be still and listen for His response)

Glory to God in the highest!

Amen

# JOY

Take delight in the Lord, and he will give
you the desires of your heart.

**Psalm 37:4**

A happy heart makes the face cheerful.

**Proverbs 15:13**

Give me happiness, O Lord, for I give myself to you.

**Psalm 86:4 NLT**

## Praying for others

Dear Almighty Father,

Please fill (insert names) with the joy that comes from Your divine and glorious love. Soften and nurture each one of their days.

May Your joy give them a window into their world. May the eyes of their hearts see all that is beautiful; may they enjoy, share and embrace life. May they know that You, Lord, are waiting for them, to sustain them; in times of trouble, in times of abundance, You are always there for them.

I ask You this in Christ's name and according to Your Holy Will.

Amen

# JOY

He will fill your mouth with laughter
and your lips with shouts of joy.

**Job 8:21**

My heart is glad and my tongue rejoices.

**Psalm 16:9**

## Praying for others

Dear Father,

Please bless (insert names) with the strength to hold onto their joy, especially during their time of need:

### (Be specific)

I pray they may be lifted up by Your mightiest Angels. Open the eyes of their hearts, Dear Lord, so that Your love and joy will fill them.

Holy Spirit, please give me the right words and timing so I may encourage and support them in a loving and Christ-like way.

### (Be still and listen)

I rejoice in Your joy, for it truly is our strength.

Amen

# HEALTH

# HEALTH

Then your light will break forth like the dawn,
and your healing will quickly appear; then
your righteousness will go before you, and the
glory of the Lord will be your rear guard.

**Isaiah 58:8**

For you who revere my name, the sun of
righteousness will rise with healing in its rays.

**Malachi 4:2**

Listen carefully to my words. Don't lose sight
of them...for they bring life to those who find
them, and healing to their whole body.

**Proverbs 4:20–22 NLT**

## Praying for myself

Almighty Father,

Fill me with the power of the Holy Spirit. Touch me with Your healing hands, and take away this illness. Release me from my pain and suffering. May I find comfort and peace in Your embrace; bless me with strength and endurance so I may faithfully demonstrate my love and devotion to You in all I say and do, despite my circumstances.

I ask You this in Your Son, Jesus Christ's name, and always, Dearest Father, according to Your perfect Holy Will.

Amen

# HEALTH

The Lord sustains them on their sickbed and
restores them from their bed of illness.

**Psalm 41:3**

Have mercy on me, Lord, for I am faint; heal me, Lord,
for my bones are in agony. My soul is in deep anguish.

**Psalm 6:2–3**

## Praying for myself

Dear Jesus,

Hear my prayer:

### (Your intention)

May my body and soul find rest and comfort today.

I know my pain and suffering are not in vain; they are such a tiny offering compared to Calvary. I come and lay my suffering at Your feet.

Lord, take hold, pull me through. It is not my strength but Yours that carries me. Touch me Dearest Savior and remove all illness.

May Your light, Your love, Your divine strength fill me completely today and every day.

Amen

# HEALTH

"I will bring health and healing... I will heal my people
and let them enjoy abundant peace and security."

**Jeremiah 33:6**

Worship the Lord your God, and his blessing
will be on your food and water. I will take
away sickness from among you.

**Exodus 23:25**

## Praying for others

Dearest Father,

I pray for the healing of:

(insert names; include as many as you wish)

May their bodies be healed by Your heavenly touch. Send Your beloved Angels to be with their families, bringing them bountiful strength, courage and endurance, and above all faith.

May the joy and love of the Holy Spirit and the grace of Your Son, Jesus Christ strengthen and comfort them.

I ask You this, according to Your Holy Will, in Your Son's name, Jesus Christ.

Amen

# HEALTH

Let all that I am praise the Lord; may I never
forget the good things he does for me. He
forgives all my sins and heals all my diseases.

**Psalm 103:2-3 NLT**

The people all tried to touch him, because power
was coming from him and healing them all.

**Luke 6:19**

## Praying for others

I ask You, Father God, in Your Son's Holy name, Jesus Christ, reach out and touch (insert names) with Your healing hands. Cleanse their bodies and rid them of all illness. Bless their minds and bodies with amazing strength and vitality

Fill them and their families with courage and endurance. Send them a miracle this day Dearest Father and move this health mountain for them.

(Reflect on their specific circumstances)

I give You thanks, Almighty God, and ask all this through Your Holy Son, Jesus Christ, according to Your perfect Will.

Amen

# WISDOM AND UNDERSTANDING

# WISDOM AND UNDERSTANDING

Whoever gives heed to instruction prospers, and
blessed is the one who trusts in the Lord.

**Proverbs 16:20**

My mouth will speak words of wisdom; the meditation
of my heart will give you understanding.

**Psalm 49:3**

### Praying for myself

Holy Spirit,

Please fill me with supreme wisdom and understanding. May my
thoughts be pure; may I be worthy of spending eternity with the
Father Almighty.

May I be fearless in expressing my honesty in all aspects of my life in
a kind and gracious way. Guide me through this wonderful life; teach
me how to demonstrate faithfully each and every day my gratitude
and love for God our Father.

### (Be still and listen to His response)

I love You, Holy Spirit, with all my heart. Fill me, guide me, show
me, direct my footsteps, in Jesus' Holy name.

Amen

# WISDOM AND UNDERSTANDING

If any of you lacks wisdom, you should ask
God, who gives generously to all without
finding fault, and it will be given to you.

**James 1:5**

I have filled him with the Spirit of God,
with wisdom, with understanding, with
knowledge and with all kinds of skills.

**Exodus 31:3**

## Praying for myself

Dear Almighty Father,

I ask You to fill me with Your Spirit. I open my heart to receive You
and all the understanding and knowledge Your Spirit so graciously
and abundantly offers me. May I use these gifts to honor and glorify
You, Father God, fulfilling Your plan for me.

Please direct my path. Look down on me from Your mighty throne
room of grace, mercy and truth. Show me Your way, Your truth, Your
light. May I always choose Your path, O Holy One, and share with
others my love for You.

(Listen to His quiet voice; what is He saying to you?)

Praise be to God.

Amen

# WISDOM AND UNDERSTANDING

The heart of the discerning acquires knowledge,
for the ears of the wise seek it out.

**Proverbs 18:15**

Give me understanding, so that I may keep
your law and obey it with all my heart.

**Psalm 119:34**

## Praying for others

Dear Jesus,

Help me to understand better (insert name) so I may be a strong and positive influence. Fill me with Your wisdom, Your strength so I may find the right words to encourage (him/her).

May (his/her) heart be open to receive the abundant blessings You so lovingly offer; gifts of wisdom, courage, joy, peace, patience and assurance. I thank You for these gifts for (insert name). May (he/she) gain confidence to humbly come before You, and ask for Your guidance, Your truth.

I praise You, Dearest Lord. I give all the glory to Your Father in Heaven, who loves us so tenderly, so completely. In Jesus' Holy name, I pray.

Amen

# WISDOM AND UNDERSTANDING

It is the spirit in a person, the breath of the
Almighty, that gives them understanding.

**Job 32:8**

The Lord gives wisdom; from his mouth comes
knowledge and understanding. For wisdom
will enter your heart, and knowledge will be
pleasant to your soul. Discretion will protect
you, and understanding will guard you.

**Proverbs 2:6,10-11**

## Praying for others

Dear God,

I pray that (insert names) be blessed with abundant understanding
and humility. May their hearts be open to receive Your wisdom,
Almighty King, faithfully fulfilling the plan You have created just
for them.

I ask the Holy Spirit to bless them with great endurance, and guide
them to the path Your love so brilliantly illuminates. Father, please
grant (insert names) strength and power through Jesus, so they may
be fearless in following You.

(Be still, listen, and meditate on God's Word above)

I ask all of this according to Your most Holy Will.

Amen

# GUIDANCE

# GUIDANCE

The Lord will guide you always; he will
satisfy your needs in a sun-scorched land
and will strengthen your frame.

**Isaiah 58:11**

The Lord directs the steps of the godly. He
delights in every detail of their lives.

**Psalm 37:23 NLT**

When he, the Spirit of truth, comes, he
will guide you into all the truth.

**John 16:13**

## Praying for myself

Dear Heavenly Father,

I ask You to bless my heart abundantly with understanding, my lips with gracious words.

I trust in You, Almighty Father, and ask the Spirit of Truth to guide my footsteps and help me navigate through life and all of its challenges. Teach me to live joyfully, to love all of Your children as You love them. Who are You laying on my heart so I can help them?

<u>(Be still and listen)</u>

I worship You, Father, and give You all the glory.

Amen

# GUIDANCE

By day the Lord went ahead of them in a pillar
of cloud to guide them on their way and by
night in a pillar of fire to give them light, so
that they could travel by day or night.

**Exodus 13:21**

He guides the humble in what is right
and teaches them his way.

**Psalm 25:9**

## Praying for myself

Dear Holy Spirit,

There are times in my life when I feel unsure of what choice to make; please guide me, fill me with confidence and knowledge.

(Tell Him what decisions you are dealing with)

I know I do not always have the answers, but I know that You do. You always have my best interest at heart; You know exactly what I need. I step back from these circumstances and give them all to You, including myself. I trust You and promise to follow You fearlessly.

(Be still and listen to what God is saying to you)

I rejoice in Your name and am so grateful for Your love and guidance. I give the Father, King of Kings, Lord of Lords, all the glory.

Amen

# GUIDANCE

In your unfailing love you will lead the people you have
redeemed. In your strength you will guide them.

**Exodus 15:13**

The Lord is my shepherd, I lack nothing...
He refreshes my soul. He guides me along
the right paths for his name's sake.

**Psalm 23:1,3**

All Scripture is inspired by God...It corrects us when
we are wrong and teaches us to do what is right.

**2 Timothy 3:16 NLT**

## Praying for others

Dear God our Father,

When I am faced with helping one of Your precious children; my
loved one (insert name), who is struggling with life's challenges,
guide me on how to best help him/her. I ask the Holy Spirit to fill me
with wisdom, understanding, and encouraging words.

## (Be still, listen)

May I be blessed with compassion and strength so I can help carry
his/her burden during this time of need.

I praise and worship You, Dearest Father. In Jesus' Holy name.

Amen

# GUIDANCE

Since you are my rock and my fortress, for the
sake of your name lead and guide me.

**Psalm 31:3**

Let the wise listen and add to their learning,
and let the discerning get guidance.

**Proverbs 1:5**

Lead me by your truth and teach me, for
you are the God who saves me.

**Psalm 25:5 NLT**

## Praying for others

Dear Jesus,

I ask in Your Holy name: please petition our Heavenly Father, to fill
(insert names) with wisdom. May the Lord guide, strengthen, and shine
His brilliant light on their path. May their earthly journey be a joyous
and loving one, serving God and serving those placed in their path.

Please help them to feel confident in coming to our Heavenly Father
for guidance, and not to be afraid to ask questions. May they find all
the right words to express their love, hopes, and concerns, knowing
in their heart that the only way to come to the Father is through You,
sweet Jesus. Guide them, Dear Lord, to make the right choices and
to open their eyes of faith to You.

Amen

# STRENGTH AND COURAGE

# STRENGTH AND COURAGE

I can do all this through him who gives me strength.

**Philippians 4:13**

"The Lord is my strength and defense; he has become
my salvation. He is my God, and I will praise him."

**Exodus 15:2**

Be strong and take heart, all you who hope in the Lord.

**Psalm 31:24**

## Praying for myself

Dear Heavenly Father,

Although I do not always understand why certain things happen, I
know I trust in You, Your love, Your ways, with all my heart.

Grant me strength, wisdom and courage to live a life in Your beloved
Son's likeness: to think like He thinks, to care like He cares, to act
as He acts.

You know my heart, Father; strengthen it, protect it, fill me with Your
divine grace.

I give You all the glory, Dearest Father, in Your Son's Holy name,
Jesus Christ. Praise be to God.

Amen

# STRENGTH AND COURAGE

My God is my rock, in whom I take refuge, my shield
and the horn of my salvation. He is my stronghold.

**2 Samuel 22:3**

Do not fear, for I am with you; do not be dismayed,
for I am your God. I will strengthen you and help you;
I will uphold you with my righteous right hand.

**Isaiah 41:10**

Stand firm in the faith; be courageous;
be strong. Do everything in love.

**1 Corinthians 16:13-14**

## Praying for myself

Dear Lord,

Give me supreme strength and courage to be successful so I may
please You by striving to live a life in the image of Your Son, Jesus
Christ. Walking through life with You inspires and encourages me
to do more, to be more. May I generously share my gifts with those
You place in my path.

I express my gratitude for the many blessings You have given me, by
using them in a way that glorifies You, Heavenly King.

(Be still, reflect on your blessings)

Amen

# STRENGTH AND COURAGE

"Be strong and courageous. The Lord your God goes
with you; he will never leave you nor forsake you."

**Deuteronomy 31:6**

"Be strong and do not give up, for
your work will be rewarded."

**2 Chronicles 15:7**

"Be strong, do not fear; your God will
come...he will come to save you."

**Isaiah 35:4**

## Praying for others

Dear Heavenly King,

I pray for (insert names); may they be blessed with enormous strength
and courage. Dear God, giver of all gifts, with the power of Your right
hand, destroy all evilness that surrounds them and bless them with a
swift, fair and peaceful resolution.

(State their circumstances)

Demolish the stronghold and restore to them their fortunes, Your
blessings, which have been stolen from them.

I lay my prayers at Your most Holy Son Jesus Christ's feet and praise
Your name. Glory be to God.

Amen

# STRENGTH AND COURAGE

"Be strong and courageous. Do not be afraid;
do not be discouraged, for the Lord your
God will be with you wherever you go."

**Joshua 1:9**

You then, my son, be strong in the
grace that is in Christ Jesus.

**2 Timothy 2:1**

## Praying for others

Dear Jesus,

I pray for (insert names), who are burdened and so weary. May they be relieved from their pain and suffering. Please Lord, help them find rest and solace in Your loving, compassionate, and caring arms. Strengthen them, Dear Lord, and fill them with immense courage, so they can face their challenges and successfully overcome them.

Grant me the strength and patience to help carry their burdens. May I embody the fruit of the Spirit in all I do, to help keep them strong and joyful despite their circumstances, which are temporary and fleeting; and You, Lord, will soon show them glory.

I ask this according to Your Heavenly Father's Holy Will. In Jesus' name, we pray.

(Be still and listen to what God tells you)

Amen

# THINKING POSITIVE

# THINKING POSITIVE

Christ will make his home in your hearts as
you trust in him. Your roots will grow down
into God's love and keep you strong.

**Ephesians 3:17 NLT**

I trust in your unfailing love; my heart
rejoices in your salvation.

**Psalm 13:5**

## Praying for myself

Dearest Father,

I humbly, yet boldly, ask You to bless me with a strong heart full
of compassion, a strong mind full of wisdom. Fill me with positive
thoughts this day and every day following. May my voice be strong,
full of uplifting words; may my body be strong, full of grace, good
health and stamina. Bless me with steady footsteps that carry forth
Your message, Your truth, Your life here on earth.

How can I serve You better? Guide me today and every day to do
Your Will.

<u>(Listen and meditate – hear God)</u>

Help me to lead by example so others may come to know You in a
personal way. All in the precious name of Your Son, Jesus.

Amen

# THINKING POSITIVE

We are hard pressed on every side, but not crushed;
perplexed, but not in despair; persecuted, but not
abandoned; struck down, but not destroyed. We always
carry around in our body the death of Jesus, so that
the life of Jesus may also be revealed in our body.

**2 Corinthians 4:8-10**

Do not let any unwholesome talk come out
of your mouths, but only what is helpful for
building others up according to their needs,
that it may benefit those who listen.

**Ephesians 4:29**

## Praying for myself

Dear Jesus,

Today and every day, I pray that I use good judgment. Guide me to show compassion, respect and humility in my thoughts, actions, words and deeds. I praise You, God for all of the wonderful blessings I have received in my life, remembering especially today:

## (What are you thankful for?)

I call upon You, Jesus, to be the Savior and Lord of my life. With You by my side, nothing is impossible. You have blessed me with love, life, redemption, and I thank You and glorify You all the days of my life.

Amen

# THINKING POSITIVE

The Lord is good to those whose hope is in
him, to the one who seeks him; it is good to
wait quietly for the salvation of the Lord.

**Lamentations 3:25-26**

For our light and momentary troubles are achieving
for us an eternal glory that far outweighs them
all. So we fix our eyes not on what is seen,
but on what is unseen, since what is seen is
temporary, but what is unseen is eternal.

**2 Corinthians 4:17-18**

## Praying for others

Dear Lord,

Remember (insert names) this day. I pray that this moment, this
challenge (be specific), does not define who they are or who they
become. May they use this hardship as an opportunity to draw close
and lean on You, to draw others close to You. Help them to understand
they are not alone; You are going through this with them. You will
never leave them.

May they see that this journey offers them many opportunities to
obtain and enjoy God's blessings through faith and trust in Him, by
way of You, Jesus. May they open their eyes and hearts to believe
and receive. Let us trust that Your ways are perfect no matter how
hard it is.

Amen

# THINKING POSITIVE

Brothers and sisters, whatever is true, whatever is
noble, whatever is right, whatever is pure, whatever
is lovely, whatever is admirable – if anything is
excellent or praiseworthy – think about such things.

## Philippians 4:8

Know that the Lord has set apart his faithful servant
for himself; the Lord hears when I call to him.

## Psalm 4:3

## Praying for others

Dear Christ Jesus,

I ask You to reach out and touch (insert names). Open their eyes to all
that awaits them. Guide them to understand and focus on the good,
the noble, the upright, and show them that through it all, they will be
profoundly blessed. May they receive Your truth, Your light. May it
shine brightly so others can see it.

I ask the Holy Spirit to fill them with love and hope. May they be
willing to walk beside You, receive Your support and guidance. Help
them to find the strength to let go of their fears. Thank You Lord, for
Your unconditional love. I rejoice in Your Holy and Blessed name.

(Tell God all the things you are thankful for)

Amen

# PATIENCE AND PERSEVERANCE

# PATIENCE AND PERSEVERANCE

Love is patient, love is kind. It always protects,
always trusts, always hopes, always perseveres.

**1 Corinthians 13:4,7**

May the Lord direct your hearts into God's
love and Christ's perseverance.

**2 Thessalonians 3:5**

### Praying for myself

Dear Father,

May everything I say, everything I do, be produced by love. May my endurance be inspired by the hope in following in Your Son Jesus Christ's footsteps and in serving Him all the days of my life.

Guide me Father. Place in my path those I need to meet and inspire with my hope.

### (Who are they? Be still and listen to God)

Shed the light, the path of truth for all to see in Jesus' Holy name.

I ask You this according to Your perfect and good Will.

Amen

# PATIENCE AND PERSEVERANCE

We boast about your perseverance and faith in all
the persecutions and trials you are enduring.

**2 Thessalonians 1:4**

Blessed is the one who perseveres under trial because,
having stood the test, that person will receive the crown
of life that the Lord has promised to those who love him.

**James 1:12**

## Praying for myself

Dear Lord,

I ask that You fill me with hope and the patience to persevere. I know that life has its ups and downs. Right now in my earthly life and home, Your objective and mine is for me to live a Christ-like life, glorifying God our Father in Heaven all the days of my life.

God has placed before me people, events, tests, miracles and glory that will help me to grow spiritually. Guide me to prepare for my heavenly home, my forever home, by doing Your work while I am here. What is Your assignment for me Lord?

### (Listen, be still - meditate)

I pray that my faith and perseverance deepens as each day passes. Thank You Lord, for being the Savior of my life.

Amen

# PATIENCE AND PERSEVERANCE

We remember before our God and Father
your work produced by faith, your labor
prompted by love, and your endurance
inspired by hope in our Lord Jesus Christ.

**1 Thessalonians 1:3**

Let perseverance finish its work so that you may
be mature and complete, not lacking anything.

**James 1:4**

## Praying for others

Dear God,

I ask that You breathe life into (insert names) and fill their hearts
with perseverance. May they feel Your presence in an amazing way.
I know that You are always nearby, but may they feel Your loving
embrace now more than ever.

May You bless them with the grace of Your Son, Jesus Christ, so that
when difficulties arise, they will hold true to their faith in You. May
they remember how far they have come instead of how far they have
to go. As Your glory sends hopelessness away, shine Your face on
them and grant them peace.

I honor and worship You, Dear Father and give You all the glory.

Amen

# PATIENCE AND PERSEVERANCE

Let us run with perseverance the race
marked out for us, fixing our eyes on Jesus,
the pioneer and perfecter of faith.

**Hebrews 12:1-2**

Being strengthened with all power according
to his glorious might so that you may
have great endurance and patience.

**Colossians 1:11**

## Praying for others

Dear Holy Spirit,

Speak to (insert names') hearts. Reveal the Lord Jesus to them, blessing them with enormous patience and perseverance. Open their eyes, ears and hearts, so they can hear Your words, Your truth, Your direction. Guide them on how to focus their lives to better serve the Almighty Father, in a glorious way.

(Be still and listen to God; what can you do to help them?)

I ask this in the name of Jesus Christ, our Lord and Redeemer, our friend, to whom I give all the glory, honor and praise.

Amen

# PEACE

# PEACE

"Blessed are the peacemakers, for they
will be called children of God."

**Matthew 5:9**

"The Lord bless you and keep you; the Lord make
his face shine on you and be gracious to you; the
Lord turn his face toward you and give you peace."

**Numbers 6:24–26**

## Praying for myself

Dearest Jesus,

I pray today I find peace all around me, a beautiful peace that soothes, calms my mind, comforts and strengthens my body. Bless me Lord with Your direction; fill me with knowledge, courage, and compassion to do the Will of Your Father. May the attitude of my heart reflect my love for You, Dear Jesus. Fill me with the fruit of the Spirit, so that I may live a life worthy of being one of Your peacemakers.

Praise You, God for You are the Mighty One who shows me love in a glorious way. I worship and honor You.

In Jesus' Holy name, I pray.

Amen

# PEACE

Let the peace of Christ rule in your hearts,
since as members of one body you were
called to peace. And be thankful.

**Colossians 3:15**

My people will live in peaceful dwelling places, in
secure homes, in undisturbed places of rest.

**Isaiah 32:18**

## Praying for myself - before I come home from ...

Dear God,

I pray there is a peace and calm as I return home today. I bind any and all evil spirits that are trying to fill my family with negativity and steal their happiness. I enter my home today with strength, love and joy in my heart as I give all I have, all I am, to You, Almighty Father.

Each morning, I vow to begin my day by wearing the Armor of God and spending quiet prayer time with You. I stand firm; I feel blessed with Your protection, firmly rooted in Your divine Word and love for me and my family.

Father, I thank You for all my many blessings, and I glorify You this day and every day of my life.

Amen

# PEACE

Grace and peace be yours in abundance through
the knowledge of God and of Jesus our Lord.

**2 Peter 1:2**

The peace of God, which transcends all understanding,
will guard your hearts and your minds in Christ Jesus.

**Philippians 4:7**

## Praying for others

Father,

I pray, believe, and receive in Your Son's name, Jesus Christ that
(insert names) will be blessed with abundant peace. May they draw
spiritual strength from You, our Heavenly and Almighty Father, as
they strive to live each day loving and serving You and those You
place in their path.

May their hearts be open to receive Your magnificent love. I pray
they will be blessed with endurance and strength for when times get
difficult. May they always keep Your Word safe in their heart and
have confidence in knowing You are always nearby.

Thank You Almighty Father. I praise and worship You.

Amen

# PEACE

May the God of hope fill you with all joy and peace
as you trust in him, so that you may overflow
with hope by the power of the Holy Spirit.

**Romans 15:13**

Grace and peace to you from God our
Father and the Lord Jesus Christ.

**Ephesians 1:2**

"The Lord your God is living among you...
With his love, he will calm all your fears."

**Zephaniah 3:17 NLT**

## Praying for others - for peace in their home

Dear Jesus,

I pray for (insert names); may they find grace and stillness in their day. May a blanket of peace fall over their homes and may all of their loved ones be blessed by Your grace with strength. I pray they are confident in knowing they can trust in You, turn to You, pray to You, and be in Your presence.

May they invite You, Jesus Christ, to come and take control of their life through the glory and love of the Holy Spirit.

Amen

# FORGIVENESS AND REDEMPTION

# FORGIVENESS AND REDEMPTION

"When you stand praying, if you hold anything
against anyone, forgive them, so that your
Father in heaven may forgive you your sins."

**Mark 11:25**

Do not remember the sins of my youth and
my rebellious ways; according to your love
remember me, for you, Lord, are good.

**Psalm 25:7**

It is by grace you have been saved, through faith –
and this is not from yourselves, it is the gift of God.

**Ephesians 2:8**

## Praying for myself

Dear Heavenly Father,

I pray, in Your Son's Holy name, Jesus Christ, for the strength, courage
and love to forgive others just as You have forgiven me. You have
thrown away all my past mistakes, and I strive to show the same love
and grace towards those who have hurt me. I will show You, Dear
Father, that in loving and forgiving them, I adore and glorify You.

I ask You this in the name of Your beloved Son, Jesus Christ, who
paid the ultimate price for my sins. I praise and worship You, Dear
Father, and rejoice in Your name.

Amen

# FORGIVENESS AND REDEMPTION

"Do not judge, and you will not be judged. Do
not condemn, and you will not be condemned.
Forgive, and you will be forgiven."

**Luke 6:37**

Put your hope in the Lord, for with the Lord is
unfailing love and with him is full redemption.

**Psalm 130:7**

## Praying for myself

Dear Father,

I know that the greatest achievement I can accomplish is to live a life
worthy of the Lord and please You in every way, all for Your glory.
My heart aches as I may fall short of glorifying You by making poor
choices. I disappoint myself, but more importantly, I let You down.
Father, I ask that You forgive me for:

### (Be specific)

Please Lord, reveal to me any sin I am holding on to, for I want to come
to You cleansed of *all* my sins. Help me to be more Christ-like in the
way I behave, think and feel. Fill me with the strength of the Holy Spirit
and the grace of Your Son, Jesus Christ. With Your guidance, I will try
harder so that You smile down on me and see how much I love You.

I glorify You, Dear Lord, and rejoice in Your Holy name.

Amen

# FORGIVENESS AND REDEMPTION

In him we have redemption through his
blood, the forgiveness of sins, in accordance
with the riches of God's grace.

**Ephesians 1:7**

Be kind and compassionate to one another, forgiving
each other, just as in Christ God forgave you.

**Ephesians 4:32**

I have swept away your sins like a cloud.

**Isaiah 44:22 NLT**

## Praying for myself

Dear Jesus, Son of God,

I come to You, admitting that I am a sinner. I bring my sins to the foot of the cross where I know You are waiting for me. I acknowledge You, Dear Jesus, and ask that You take away my hurt and heal my heart. Cleanse me with Your grace and take my prayers to Your Father and ask Him to forgive me.

Grant me humility, compassion and strength to forgive others, as Our Father forgives me. May my mind hold forgiving thoughts, my mouth forgiving words and my body forgiving actions. You are the Savior of my life, and I honor and adore You.

Amen

# FORGIVENESS AND REDEMPTION

All are justified freely by his grace through
the redemption that came by Christ Jesus.

**Romans 3:24**

He has rescued us from the dominion of darkness and
brought us into the kingdom of the Son he loves, in
whom we have redemption, the forgiveness of sins.

**Colossians 1:13-14**

## Praying for myself

Dear Heavenly Father,

Your Son's dying breath brought us life. Through His suffering; we were saved. How great is Your love Dearest Father, to have given Your only Son, to save our souls and bless us with the glorious inheritance of the riches of Your love and eternal life.

I pray we are all able to take our sins to the cross, to ask for forgiveness and to bring home with us the redemption that awaits us. May we forgive ourselves and look ahead, inviting You to fill us with great faith and perseverance.

I show You the attitude of my heart by striving to serve You in a loving, obedient way. I praise You, Dearest Father, and rejoice in Your Son's Blessed name, Jesus Christ.

Amen

# FEAR AND ANXIETY

# FEAR AND ANXIETY

Do not be anxious about anything, but in
every situation, by prayer and petition, with
thanksgiving, present your requests to God.

**Philippians 4:6**

The Lord is my light and my salvation - whom
shall I fear? The Lord is the stronghold of my
life - of whom shall I be afraid?

**Psalm 27:1**

## Praying for myself

Holy Spirit,

Please fill me with Your abundant peace. Quiet my mind and ease my
fear. I ask for Your supreme guidance and intervention.

### (What is on your mind, in your heart?)

Obliterate this evilness and darkness that surround me. Let me feel
Your presence; walk with me and strengthen me as I work through life's
challenges. I know I will face trials and tribulations of many kinds. May
I handle each one of them in a way that glorifies our Father in Heaven.

### (Be still and hear what God has to say)

I ask You all this, with a heart full of gratitude and love. Your Grace
is sufficient.

Amen

# FEAR AND ANXIETY

Humble yourselves, therefore, under God's mighty
hand, that he may lift you up in due time. Cast all
your anxiety on him because he cares for you.

**1 Peter 5:6-7**

Even though I walk through the darkest valley,
I will fear no evil, for you are with me.

**Psalm 23:4**

## Praying for myself

Almighty Father,

Please fill my heart with strength and courage.

May the Grace and peace of Your Son, Jesus Christ, calm my thoughts
in times of concern. Deepen my faith; You are always beside me.

## (Give God all your worries)

May Your grace meet my fears and quiet them. May Your strength
cast away all worries, doubt, fear and anxiety.

## (Meditate on God's Word above)

I praise You in Jesus' Holy name, Dear Father, and give You all the
glory.

Amen

# FEAR AND ANXIETY

Truly my soul finds rest in God; my salvation comes
from him. Truly he is my rock and my salvation;
he is my fortress, I will never be shaken.

**Psalm 62:1-2**

"I am the God of your father Abraham. Do not
be afraid, for I am with you; I will bless you."

**Genesis 26:24**

Do not throw away your confidence;
it will be richly rewarded.

**Hebrews 10:35**

## Praying for others

Dear Father,

Today, I pray for (insert names). May their fears and anxieties be calmed; may their trust and faith in You be deeply rooted.

I pray they allow You to lead the way for them, Your mighty and comforting love illuminating their path through a brilliant life filled with hope, courage and love. May their heart be always open to receive Your blessed and glorious Word: the true food, seed for their soul that nurtures and sustains, growing in them always.

I praise You Dearest Father and rejoice in Your Holy name.

Amen

# FEAR AND ANXIETY

"I will grant peace in the land, and you will lie
down and no one will make you afraid."

**Leviticus 26:6**

"Do not be afraid of them, for I am with you
and will rescue you," declares the Lord.

**Jeremiah 1:8**

We say with confidence, "The Lord is
my helper; I will not be afraid."

**Hebrews 13:6**

## Praying for others

Dearest Father,

I pray that (insert names) will be delivered from all their worries and
fears. May they be blessed with the wisdom and strength to walk the
path that You have set out for them.

May they work hard to build a stronger, solid relationship with You
and Your Blessed Son, Jesus Christ, showing enormous faith in
giving up the fight to be in control. May they place their trust in You.
Help them to surrender all their fears, believing firmly that with You
in control, nothing can be out of control.

I ask You all this, according to Your Holy perfect Will.

Amen

# NOT DWELLING ON THE PAST

# NOT DWELLING ON THE PAST

"Forget the former things; do not dwell on the past."

**Isaiah 43:18**

Jesus replied, "No one who puts a hand to the plow and looks back is fit for service in the kingdom of God."

**Luke 9:62**

## Praying for myself

Dear Jesus,

When I accept You as my Savior, You make all things new. Help me not to look back at my life and recollect unpleasant things that have happened. Grant me the compassion and supreme love to forgive those who have hurt me or those I love, for if I can't find forgiveness in my heart, how can I ask for forgiveness from You? How can I move forward if I can't let go of the past?

### (Listen for God's answer, His direction, His truth)

Please instill in me the confidence and resolve not to let guilt, resentment, anger or the expectations of others affect who I am. Shift my thinking, Dear Jesus, to let go of any thoughts that hold me back. My Lord and Savior, save me from myself.

I ask You as a faithful child of God, and I give our Almighty Father all the praise and glory forever.

Amen

# NOT DWELLING ON THE PAST

Set your hearts on things above, where Christ is,
seated at the right hand of God. Set your minds
on things above, not on earthly things.

## Colossians 3:1-2

Forgetting what is behind and straining toward what is
ahead, I press on toward the goal to win the prize for
which God has called me heavenward in Christ Jesus.

## Philippians 3:13-14

## Praying for myself

Dear God,

As I work through my weaknesses, please help me to turn them into
strengths for Your glory. Fill me with courage and compassion, so
I can learn to forgive myself of my past mistakes; push me to move
forward in a bright and beautiful way.

### (Reflect what is heavy on your heart)

Thank You, Father, for loving me and believing in me. From this
day forward, I will strive to not look back; I will start each day with
asking You, "What do I need to do today to serve You better?" Bless
me God with the grace of Your Son, Jesus Christ.

### (Be still and listen, meditate on God's Word and hear Him)

Amen

# NOT DWELLING ON THE PAST

Because of his great love for us, God, who
is rich in mercy, made us alive with Christ
even when we were dead in transgressions –
it is by grace you have been saved.

**Ephesians 2:4-5**

Throw off your old sinful nature and your former
way of life...let the Spirit renew your thoughts
and attitudes. Put on your new nature, created
to be like God – truly righteous and holy.

**Ephesians 4:22-24 NLT**

## Praying for myself

Dear Holy Father,

When I find myself reflecting on the past in a way that makes me feel bad, regretful, questioning why things happened, I am reminded that it is Satan who tries to make me feel like a failure. With the strength of Your Son, Jesus Christ, I resist his attempts to steal my happiness and most importantly Your Word from my heart. I turn around and tell him that he has no authority over me, that Your beloved Son Jesus died for me so that I might be made righteous through faith in Him.

(What do you want to let go of; give it to Jesus)

I will not get discouraged. I will set my face like flint and look toward Jesus: His way, His truth.

Amen

# NOT DWELLING ON THE PAST

The light shines in the darkness, and the
darkness has not overcome it.

**John 1:5**

Life will be brighter than noonday, and
darkness will become like morning. You will
be secure, because there is hope; you will look
about you and take your rest in safety.

**Job 11:17–18**

If anyone is in Christ, the new creation has
come: The old has gone, the new is here!

**2 Corinthians 5:17**

## Praying for others

Almighty Father,

I pray for (insert names); may they have immense courage and
strength to look forward to the bright and beautiful future You have
planned for them. May they feel confident, believing they were made
for so much more than what has happened in their past.

Bring them healing, Father. Lift them up and fortify them with the
strength always to trust in You, knowing that You will always direct
and nurture their heart if they give themselves fully to You, allowing
You to lead. Wherever You lead is always the right direction. May
the grace of our Lord, Jesus Christ, be with all of us.

Amen

# AFFLICTION AND ADVERSITY

# AFFLICTION AND ADVERSITY

You became imitators of us and of the Lord, for
you welcomed the message in the midst of severe
suffering with the joy given by the Holy Spirit.

**1 Thessalonians 1:6**

Be joyful in hope, patient in affliction, faithful in prayer.

**Romans 12:12**

### Praying for myself

Almighty Father,

Bless me with enormous courage and perseverance. May I feel Your presence now more than ever as I pray to You for:

<u>(What areas do you need help with; tell God)</u>

As I move forward, free me from this bondage. Grant me the grace to grow abundantly in faith, joy, hope, and love. Guide me Dear Father. May I be fearless in these times of adversity, trusting confidently in Your amazing love.

May the Holy Spirit walk with me so I can lean on Him for strength. May my faith and trust in You be ever-growing.

I ask You all this, in the name of Christ, Your beloved Son, and as always, according to Your Holy Will.

Amen

# AFFLICTION AND ADVERSITY

In all this you greatly rejoice, though now for a little
while you may have had to suffer grief in all kinds of
trials. These have come so that the proven genuineness
of your faith – of greater worth than gold...may result in
praise, glory and honor when Jesus Christ is revealed.

**1 Peter 1:6-7**

Consider it pure joy, my brothers and sisters, whenever
you face trials of many kinds, because you know that
the testing of your faith produces perseverance.

**James 1:2- 3**

## Praying for myself

Dear Jesus,

The love of Your Father pours into my heart through the Holy Spirit.
I receive all of Him and praise God for the joy I feel in being loved
by You, eternal love which has no boundaries.

Dear Lord, I thank You for saving and redeeming me. Guide me
today and every day, as I offer up all my adversities in the hope of
glorifying Your Father.

(What are your adversities; what can God help you with?)

Shed the light, the path of truth for all to see, in Your Holy name.

Amen

# AFFLICTION AND ADVERSITY

If you will seek God earnestly and plead with the Almighty, if you are pure and upright, even now he will rouse himself on your behalf and restore you to your prosperous state.

**Job 8:5-6**

Cast your cares on the Lord and he will sustain you; he will never let the righteous be shaken.

**Psalm 55:22**

## Praying for others

Holy Father,

May the grace of Your Son, Jesus Christ, be with (insert names). Grant them strength and courage so they may stand firm in their faith and love for You, Dearest Father. May they never give up hope. I pray that Your loving light illuminates the darkness they may feel during this time of challenge.

Through Your Spirit God, move this mountain for them:

(What is their mountain? Health, finances, relationship, etc)

May they overflow with hope by the power of the Holy Spirit and honor You in all ways.

I ask You this in Your beloved Son's name, Jesus Christ.

Amen

# AFFLICTION AND ADVERSITY

The eyes of the Lord are on the righteous,
and his ears are attentive to their cry. The
righteous cry out, and the Lord hears them;
he delivers them from all their troubles.

**Psalm 34:15,17**

"The Lord will fight for you; you need only to be still."

**Exodus 14:14**

## Praying for others

Dear Jesus,

I humbly ask You to grant (insert names) strength. Bless them with infinite wisdom and courage to handle life's challenges especially:

(How can God help them?)

I pray with all my heart that they are successful in triumphing over their adversity through Your love and grace. May their faith grow ever so abundantly, and may the peace and grace of the Holy Spirit blanket their household. I thank You, Dear Lord, for hearing my prayer and petitions. I honor and glorify You.

Amen

# PROTECTION

# PROTECTION

In peace I will lie down and sleep, for you
alone, Lord, make me dwell in safety.

**Psalm 4:8**

For he will command his angels concerning you to guard
you in all your ways; they will lift you up in their hands,
so that you will not strike your foot against a stone.

**Psalm 91:11-12**

## Prayer for myself

Dear Jesus,

I pray I am strong, and my heart is always open and full of God's Holy Word.

May I be blessed with the courage to persevere and live each day to serve and glorify our most Holy Father.

Bless my days with joy in the knowledge of Your love through all spiritual wisdom and understanding, so that each day I can become more like You.

(Be still, listen to what God tells you)

Bless my nights with security, peace and blissful serenity that soothes my soul. Shine Your face upon me, Dear Jesus and keep me safe.

Amen

# PROTECTION

May your love and faithfulness always protect me.

**Psalm 40:11**

When you walk, your steps will not be hampered;
when you run, you will not stumble.

**Proverbs 4:12**

You, Lord, will keep the needy safe and will
protect us forever from the wicked.

**Psalm 12:7**

## Prayer for myself

Dear Father,

I pray for the strength and wisdom not to fall into temptation. May the Spirit of God guide me each day to walk in the Spirit, faithfully focusing on pleasing You in all I do, all I say, all I am, Dearest Father.

Protect me against evil, against negativity, Lord, and please bless me with abundant courage and perseverance, today and every day, as I strive to live a life worthy of spending eternity with You.

I ask You this according to Your Holy Will and give You all the glory and honor. In Jesus' Holy name I pray.

Amen

# PROTECTION

You, Lord, are my lamp; the Lord turns my
darkness into light. It is God who arms me
with strength and keeps my way secure.

**2 Samuel 22:29,33**

Let all who take refuge in you be glad; let them ever
sing for joy. Spread your protection over them, that
those who love your name may rejoice in you.

**Psalm 5:11**

## Praying for others

Sweet Holy Spirit,

I ask You today to protect (insert names). Watch over them with Your loving eyes and guide their footsteps.

Place a blanket of love, peace and safety over their household and over all those whom they love. Strengthen their trust in You and protect them from negativity, evil, and temptation.

May their heart be always open to receive You, embracing Your love.

I praise the Almighty Father for His bountiful blessings and His supreme love.

Glory to God in the highest.

Amen

# PROTECTION

"Whoever listens to me will live in safety
and be at ease, without fear of harm."

**Proverbs 1:33**

You will go on your way in safety, and your foot will
not stumble. When you lie down, you will not be
afraid; when you lie down, your sleep will be sweet.

**Proverbs 3:23-24**

"The Lord's word is flawless; he shields
all who take refuge in him."

**2 Samuel 22:31**

## Praying for others

Dear Father,

I pray for (insert names) to be blessed with enormous strength. I ask You to protect their hearts, binding all negativity and evilness that may try to hurt them. May Your divine love protect them and guide their footsteps.

May the Holy Spirit fill them with confidence and courage to bravely face each day, keeping Your Word tucked safely in their hearts as they strive to live a life pleasing to You, Dear Lord.

I adore and glorify You, Almighty King and in Jesus' Holy name I pray.

Amen

# EPILOGUE

Part I of *PRAYER MADE SIMPLE* contains the lessons I learned during a time of hardship my family recently endured. These lessons combined with daily prayer changed my life. They can change yours too!

These hardships could have easily destroyed my family in one way or another. I chose to pray, worship, and place my love, trust, faith, and prayers with God our Father. I turned my life joyfully over to Him – surrendered it *all*, so He could move my mountains; and that is just what God did.

Believe me when I say that not every day was easy, and yes, those hardships changed me forever - *for the better!* Every lesson learned was priceless and has become an integral part of who I am today and who I strive to be.

The Holy Spirit continues to be with me each and every day, guiding me, loving me, helping me to focus daily on the plan God has set out for me. I know in my heart that the Holy Spirit guided me to write this book in the face of my adversity to share with you how to pray, believe, and trust in God for guidance.

I hope *PRAYER MADE SIMPLE* will encourage you to open up a dialogue with God by turning the pages of your Bible. Read and feel His Word; pray to Him, speak to Him, listen to Him and most importantly, embrace and live His perfect plan for *your* life. God is waiting to answer your prayers, to move the mountains in *your* life.

# RESOURCES

While writing this book, I cannot tell you how many times I thought, "Everyone should have a Pam Watson in their life!" She has been an incredible inspiration to me. Pam's love and faith in God our Father; her wisdom, understanding, and her sweet heart – full of pure and humble intentions, all to glorify and serve the Lord – helped me to bring this book to life. I am so grateful. I gladly share her ministry with you in hopes that one day your paths might cross; what a true blessing it will be!

Pam Watson
**PSW Ministries**
PSWATSON@AOL.COM
239-348-2500 (phone)
239-261-1814 (fax)

# ABOUT THE AUTHOR

Terry Manley is a dedicated Christian who believes that prayer is our lifeline to God. She is not a famous author; in fact, this is her first book. Nor is she a scholar with formal Biblical training that would qualify her to write a book about God and prayer. She does not have a "teacher" in the earthly sense, but she does have the best teachers any and all of us could ever have: The Bible and the Holy Spirit.

She has experienced for herself and witnessed for others many answered prayers that have changed her life.

"What is impossible with man is possible with God."

**Luke 18:27**

Terry was born and raised in New Jersey, and now resides in Southwest Florida with her husband, Steve, and their dog, Jack. She boards her horse, America, at a nearby stable, adjacent to a beautiful state forest. Terry enjoys riding its endless trails, feeling especially close to God while surrounded by the beauty of His vast woodlands.

If *PRAYER MADE SIMPLE* has been helpful to you, Terry would love to hear your story of how God has changed your life. She may be contacted at TerryManley@me.com or visit her website: www. TerryManley.com

# NOTES

1   Watson, Pam. *PSW Ministries,* Personal interview, 3 Mar. 2014.

2   Warren, Rick. *The Purpose Driven Life,* (Grand Rapids: Zondervan, 2012), 103.

3   Hinn, Benny. *Good Morning Holy Spirit,* (Nashville: Thomas Nelson, 2004), 47-49, 67.

4   Hinn, 54.

5   "PERSONAL ATTRIBUTES OF THE HOLY SPIRIT." *GodOnThe.Net, n.d.* ‹http://www.godonthe.net/HolySpirit/ques›, Aug. 2014.

6   Warren, 34, 173.

7   Hinn, 50, 53.

8   "The Work of the Holy Spirit." *Truthnet, n.d.* ‹http://www.truthnet.org/Holy-Spirit/1HolySpirit-work/Index.htm›, 8 July 2014.

9   Warren, 84.

10  Hinn, 47-48.

11  Warren, 84.

12  "What does it mean to surrender to God?" *Got Questions Ministries, n.d.* ‹http://www.gotquestions.org/surrender-to-God.html›, 17 Aug. 2014.

13  Warren, 102.

14  Richards, Fr. Larry. "The Power of the Holy Spirit." *Those Catholic Men, n.d.* ‹http://thosecatholicmen.com/the-power-of-the-holy-spirit/›, 17 Aug. 2014.

15  Warren, 80.

16  Warren, 47.

17  Warren, 172-73.

18  Warren, 180-81.

19  Warren, 89.

20  Bailey, Dr. Bill. "Why Speak Your Faith? *Word of Faith Ministries, Inc." n.d.* ‹http://speakfaith.com/articles/why_speak_your_faith.html›, 5 July 2014.

21  Watson

22  Savelle, Jerry. *If Satan Can't Steal Your Joy...He Can't Keep Your Goods*, (Tulsa: Harrison House, 2002), 128-131.

23  Bailey

24  "What is the full armor of God?" *Got Questions Ministries*, n.d. ‹http://www.gotquestions.org/full-armor-of-God.html›, 10 May 2014.

25  Warren, 213-14.

26  Rev. Linda Smallwood, "Standing in the Gap?" What Does That Mean? *My Redeemer Lives Christian Ministry n.d.* ‹http://www.myredeemerlives.com/intercession.html›, 2 July 2014.

27  Bailey

28  Warren, 200.

29  Warren, 208.

30  Savelle, 40.

31  Savelle, 45.

32  Savelle, 143.